Life's Too Short to Date Men Like Me

Life's Too Short to Date Men Like Me

Willie Booker

iUniverse, Inc.
Bloomington

Life's Too Short to Date Men Like Me

The information, ideas, and suggestions in this book are not intended as a substitute for professional advice. Before following any suggestions contained in this book, you should consult your personal physician or mental health professional. Neither the author nor the publisher shall be liable or responsible for any loss or damage allegedly arising as a consequence of your use or application of any information or suggestions in this book.

iUniverse books may be ordered through booksellers or by contacting:

iUniverse
1663 Liberty Drive
Bloomington, IN 47403
www.iuniverse.com
1-800-Authors (1-800-288-4677)

Because of the dynamic nature of the Internet, any web addresses or links contained in this book may have changed since publication and may no longer be valid. The views expressed in this work are solely those of the author and do not necessarily reflect the views of the publisher, and the publisher hereby disclaims any responsibility for them.

Any people depicted in stock imagery provided by Thinkstock are models, and such images are being used for illustrative purposes only.
Certain stock imagery © Thinkstock.

ISBN: 978-1-4620-4272-2 (sc)
ISBN: 978-1-4620-4273-9 (hc)
ISBN: 978-1-4620-4274-6 (ebk)

Library of Congress Control Number: 2011913458

Printed in the United States of America

iUniverse rev. date: 08/03/2011

Contents

This book is dedicated to everyone I've hurt over the years. I'm truly sorry for all that I did. This book won't fix things, but I hope it'll bring you all a little laughter.

Introduction

A few months prior to completing this book I almost died. My head was about to split in half from altitude sickness, and I was freezing my butt off. Not a surprise because I was at an altitude of 5,400meters, in a place called Thorung La Pass somewhere high up in the mountains in Nepal.

It had taken me over a week to hike up there, and maybe it was due to the thin air, but I wasn't thinking straight and was contemplating staying overnight, to freeze to death at the top of the world, because loneliness and guilt had finally caught up with me for all the awful things I had done in my life, and that included taking for granted every woman who ever loved me.

For an hour I sat there looking at the amazing scenery, and then I dragged myself off of that mountain, because I knew staying would hurt even more people by causing grief to my family and friends. So I came back to complete this book, a project that I had started before I had gone to Nepal.

Now, I don't want you to read this thinking this book is going to be about some suicidal weirdo. This book is about men, relationships, and how to deal with men, and I hope this book will crack you and your friends up and help you in the process.

The reason I'm disclosing that I once contemplated suicide is because I want to show that I am sincere and have nothing to hide.

Although the average asshole lies, manipulates and tries to protect his reputation even when he does the shittiest things, I have nothing to lose by telling you what went on in my life. After all, what could be worse than freezing to death on a mountain?

Just look at the title of this book, which says it all: I am an asshole! After this book is published, I'll be surprised if women touch me with a six-foot pole. I'll probably have to spend the rest of my life watching porn in the basement and making love to a blow-up doll, and that's a fate I'm prepared to face.

I'm going to tell you the truth, and on top of that I spent years partying with all sorts of guys, from the nice guys to the players and every type in between. I know what makes us tick, what we want in women and the tricks that we use, and I can explain this in a systematic way. Basically, I can reveal everything you need to know about men, something the average asshole would never do.

Maybe some good can come out of the life of an asshole. I can offer truth when most guys just offer bullshit. So if you really want to understand men better, then keep reading.

PART 1

How to Spot and Avoid Assholes

Chapter 1

Where All the Good Men Went

I can't even recall how it all started, but it was years before this book even became a concept. Female friends would come to me for relationship advice; sometimes they came to me distraught, wondering why their relationships failed or why men treated them badly. For years I tried to fix their problems and called the men they dated jerks and assholes. Then one day a rather inconvenient realization hit me in the gut like a well aimed punch.

My female friends were coming to me for advice because I was just as bad as many of the men they were dating. That's when I decided it was a good idea to teach women to avoid assholes like myself and how to attract decent men, and I knew the only effective way to do it was by explaining the truth without sugar coating any of it.
So I apologize if the language in this book is blunt, and crude at times, but the only way you're ever going to understand men is if you learn how to put yourself in a man's shoes .

A common problem for many women these days is that there seems to be fewer and fewer decent men out there. Every guy they meet is either a creepy loser or some game playing scumbag. To explain why there are so many losers and jerks out there, you have to first read a passage that's been floating around the Internet for years:

In a brief conversation, a man asked a woman he was pursuing the question, "What kind of man are you looking for?"

She sat quietly for a moment before looking him in the eye and asking, "Do you really want to know?"

Reluctantly, he said "yes."

She began to expound, "As a woman in this day and age, I am in a position to ask a man what he can do for me that I can't do for myself. I pay my own bills. I take care of my household without the help of any man, or woman for that matter. I am in the position to ask, 'What can you bring to the table?'"

The man looked at her. Clearly he thought that she was referring to money. She quickly corrected his thought and stated, "I am not referring to money. I need something more. I need a man who is striving for perfection in every aspect of life."

He sat back in his chair, folded his arms, and asked her to explain.

She said, "I am looking for someone who is striving for perfection mentally because I need conversation and mental stimulation. I don't need a simple-minded man. I am looking for someone who is striving for perfection spiritually because I don't need to be unequally yoked. Believers mixed with unbelievers is a recipe for disaster. I need a man who is striving for perfection financially because I don't need a financial burden."

"I am looking for someone who is sensitive enough to understand what I go through as a woman, but strong enough to keep me grounded. I am looking for someone whom I can respect. In order to be submissive, I must respect him. I cannot be submissive to a man who isn't taking care of his business. I have no problem being submissive; he just has to be worthy. God made woman to be a help mate for man. I can't help a man if he can't help himself."

When she finished her spiel, she looked at him. He sat there with a puzzled look on his face. He said, "You're asking a lot."

She replied, "I'm worth a lot."

My response:

The fantasy:

- The man is perfect in every aspect of his life
- Perfect mentally
- Good at conversation
- Spiritual (guess that's important if you're spiritual)
- Financially perfect (or striving for it)
- Knows what a woman goes through
- Sensitive
- Someone that can be respected
- She forgot to add, faithful, not butt ugly, and relatively tall.

But the reality:

Such a man, if he exists, is either gay or in a relationship already, because if he's that special, you can be sure his girlfriend or wife guards him like the Holy Grail and will fend off all you other girls from a mile away.

The other 99 percent of men out there lack most of these qualities:

Perfect Mentally: What the hell does this mean anyway? I've heard of smart, but perfect mentally? I know plenty of guys who are totally mental. Is that anything close?

Good at Conversation: Most guys are full of brain farts, or they're full of shit. If a guy is a really smooth talker you can be sure he's trying to sweet talk multiple girls into bed.

Spiritual: I respect religion so I won't mess around with this. But a lot of girls can't even find a nice guy yet they are sure they can find a spiritual guy who's got the other qualities?

Financially Perfect: Again what does this mean? If it means what I think it means, then she's referring to the likes of Bill Gates and Donald Trump. Are you sure you want to have a relationship with a nerd or a stuck-up asshole with a really bad hair-cut? The rest of us fall somewhere between "imperfect but able to buy a house" to "some dish washer in the back of a restaurant."

Knows What a Woman Goes Through: He must be gay.

Sensitive: Gay or a player trying to get into your pants.

Someone Who Can Be Respected: Most men are either; emasculated and weak versions of our former, hunter, warrior race. Which is why women call them nice guys, pat them on the back, "friend zone" them and then complain there are no nice guys.

Or,

They're strong, don't get pushed around, don't grovel for a woman's attention, are not needy, are not clingy, respect themselves. But they're sleeping around.

Physical Aspects: As for the rest of men, they're either too short, look like a car ran over their face, or their penis are so small when they put it in the girl asks "Is it in yet?"

The reality is we're not perfect. The above list is the equivalent of a man asking for a super hot girl with a perfect body who is smart, has a nice personality, has a good sense of humor, is caring, is not a gold digger, and is willing to cook, clean and hand wash the skid marks off of our underwear. Do you really think that's realistic?

Okay, I know what the deal is. The majority of girls want a high-quality male, and there's nothing wrong with that. The problem is whether you like it or not, most guys are pretty average, and the high-quality males out there get so much female attention they have the option to play around(even if they don't act upon it).

Someone once told me the top 10 percent of men date about 50 percent of women, the next 50 percent of men date the other 50 percent of women, and 40 percent of men struggle to get dates or female attention at all.

Whether you like it or not that's probably pretty close to the reality in society. There's more demand for attractive males than there is supply. Although I think all women deserve a great guy, the fact that there aren't enough great guys to go around means all of you getting one is a mathematical impossibility. That means if a woman wants her Prince Charming who's a good catch, then she has to be willing to share (yeah right), or she's got to compete and beat the rest of the girls to get him.

This is why it feels like there are very few good men out there: they're taken already. Some women stay single, some always seem to end up with the jerks, and others get the guys they want, and it's not because of luck. I'll explain later some of the things these women did to get the men they really wanted.

Chapter 2

The Most Important Differences between Men and Women

There are women who have one-night stands all the time, and there are men who are desperate to get married. But it doesn't take a rocket scientist to figure out that generally men and women view relationships differently with regards to commitment.

A large part of this comes from animal instinct, and you can see it in other mammal species: males want to spread their seed, whereas females prefer a strong and steady partner that will stick around to help raise the young.

If you ask your female friends, "Would you date someone that you liked, but you know you will definitely break up six months later, and there's no chance of a future together?" Most will say no, because there's not even the slightest chance of a future together, and breaking up sucks. But ask guys the same question, and a lot would say yes.

Why? Well, there's no future, but there's sex! Some guys might even spend all their time pursuing such relationships. So here's the first important difference (Although not all guys are like this, many are):

1) A guy doesn't need to like a girl to have sex with her, and he might put a lot of effort into chasing just for sex.

You could say a lot of girls can have sex without feelings, but the key difference is that even if a girl has a one-night stand, she needs to see something interesting in a guy. He was probably confident, interesting to talk to, or at least had something going for him. If a girl is not interested, she will simply brush the guy aside.

Guys don't need to feel any interest beyond the physical, and sometimes it's still a go. Not interested but she's attractive enough.... sex. Not attracted but one too many beers .... sex. Trying to score all night but crash and burned ten times and will settle for anything walking on two legs .... sex. Governor of New York, married with kids, and needs to pay top dollar .... sex. President of the United States .... wait, my bad, oral sex doesn't count!

It's gross, I know, but then you're a girl! Even if women like sex too, they don't feel the same constant horniness men feel. The closest I can describe a man's sex drive is that it's like having an addiction that needs to be fed all the time. Just imagine you haven't eaten for twenty-four hours, and a succulent buffet with the best meats, salads, chocolates, and desserts is laid out in front of you. Your eagerness for that food will probably match an average man's lust for sex.

Sure, women know that men want sex a lot, but I think most women still underestimate how much men will do just to get sex. Not all men are dogs, but when a guy's an asshole, he'll lie and do whatever it takes to get a woman interested. What confuses some women is when a guy puts in a lot of effort to chase her and sweet talk her; she thinks he genuinely likes her and is not just after sex. That's when a woman gets played.

A lot of people wrongly assume the opposite sex has similar desires and will act in a similar way. A lot of women assume just because they wouldn't lie, act all nice and sweet, and spend tons of time and money just to get sex, a man wouldn't do the same. Oh how wrong.

The other important difference and this gets women hurt even more is this:

2) A guy might not see any future (or want any future) with a girl, but he'll still date her and even treat her well, and the whole time she's hoping there will be a future.

Women hate when men waste their time and ultimately break their hearts. If a woman doesn't like a man anymore, unless she's married to the guy with kids, she'll usually dump the guy pretty quickly.

Men often lead women on. Why?

Well, first of all there's you guessed it. Sex! Then there's the fact that it's nice to have steady company, even if the guy doesn't want to take it any further. There are also guys who are chicken shit and scared to dump a girl, and they drag it on forever.

But probably the worst thing about assholes such as myself is that we're actually capable of falling in love, or at least feeling infatuation. We might be assholes, but we're still human after all. It's just that we also fall out of love like the changing of the seasons. The only person we truly love is ourselves; everyone else comes and goes.

Very few jerks set out to deliberately hurt a girl. A lot of jerks are either selfish people or are ignorant of the effects of their unwillingness to commit to a proper relationship. Every asshole you ever dated probably did like you in some lukewarm way but not enough to bring you the happiness that you want or feel like you deserve in your life. So again, would you date a guy if you knew before hand there definitely would be no future? Would you still make the same choice before you got emotionally attached? The answer is most likely no.

Oh yeah women hate men like us, but once women understand how assholes operate, all it takes is time and careful observation to spot one. So here's one difference between men and women that a lot of women don't take enough advantage of.

3) Women get to pick men.

It's amazing that when I discuss this point with female friends, some never thought about it that way. A lot of them think men and women pick each other. Err no, you have probably had dozens of men hit on you over the years, and you weren't interested and brushed them off; you might not even have noticed they were flirting with you and just walked off and the guy gave up.

Women and men might decide to start a life together later in the relationship, but women pick men at the start. Men notice this a lot more than women, because men hit on women and get rejected all the time. If we come on too strong, we're desperate; if we talk too much about boring subjects, we're annoying; if we're in a girl's face all the time, we're clingy, and the guy who just keeps looking but is too scared to make a move is surely a stalking serial killer!

Women get to pick men, and all women have to do is figure out (A) if a man's worthy enough, if he's perfect in every way (refer back to chapter one), and (B) if he's going to treat her right.

A lot of women are very good at (A) and really bad at (B), and that's why they get hurt over and over again. They meet a guy who's attractive and hitting on them, and they lose their minds. Lots of women meet a guy they're attracted to and make a decision on the guy way too soon. That won't happen again after reading this book; if you learn what I know and know what to look for then it's pretty easy to dodge the assholes out there.

Chapter 3

How to Deal with Players

Most people would define a player as someone who has multiple sex partners and has no moral scruples about it. I see players as something different altogether. Players are like recreational drugs: women do players only because they were attracted and it felt good at the beginning, but one too many hits and there's the potential to get hooked.

Let's be honest, a guy can only attract lots of women and play around if he's got something going for him. If a guy is short, weighs four hundred pounds, and is stupid, and boring to talk to, he's not going to have sex with many females. Yes that's right. The guy who coined the phrase "Beauty is in the eye of the beholder" was obviously not very attractive, and was trying to make himself feel better.

But it's not just based on looks. Although there are very few ugly players, not all players are good looking; that's a mistake a lot of women make. A lot of women fear dating handsome men because they think these men attract a lot of women. But if that's the case then male models would attract more women than average-looking celebrities and rich men, and they don't. Just think of Mick Jagger or Steven Tyler; they fell off the ugly tree and hit every branch on the way down, but they still had tons of women interested in them.

The attributes that are synonymous with players are confidence, fun, and the ability to make a woman feel attracted through the use of words. When women think of players, they generally feel disdain, but that's neglecting a very important fact about players: they are attractive, and it's a fatal type of attraction so don't underestimate that.

So what are the early red flags that you're dealing with a typical player?

1) Players are always very confident, and most women find confidence attractive. After all, confidence is one of the probable indicators of success. It doesn't mean that women need to avoid all confident men and go for nervous wrecks, but over confidence means the guy isn't worried about rejection and doesn't actually like the girl. When a guy truly likes a girl he'll usually show some hesitation and awkwardness around her.

2) They have excellent conversation skills. This makes them interesting to talk to, but contrary to popular belief, players don't lay on lots of compliments early on. That only comes off as having an agenda, and good players are never obvious. Players often say the right things because they actually put an effort into listening to what a girl has to say, and that's why it makes a girl feel special.

3) Players are fun to be with and often have a good sense of humor. That poses a problem for women, because a person who's funny and fun to be with is naturally attractive. It doesn't mean a funny guy is definitely going to be a player. The problem is fun and humor are naturally disarming, and it's hard to picture a guy who's making you laugh as an asshole in a relationship. Unfortunately fun and commitment have zero correlation.

4) A normal guy is scared to touch a girl early on, because he's scared of rejection. Players are usually pretty touchy from the start and this is to do with boldness and confidence.

Good players are also good at reading women and only start touching a woman when they notice a woman's already attracted. An arm around the shoulder, an arm around the waist, on your lower back, even on your butt. There are three reasons why players are touchy. (A) They want to touch you. (B) They can test your interest level; if you don't pull away, then they can escalate the amount of contact and where they touch. (C) If you're already attracted, then touch is a turn-on, especially when you've been drinking.

5) Pushing for sex. The idea that if a girl doesn't have sex with a guy by the third date she's playing games and being a dick tease was obviously created by a player. Modern dating practices are a boon for players because women often feel if they don't put out fast enough, the guy will run. But if a guy is pushing a girl to have sex and is not willing to wait, it's not because he's getting blue balls or really wants the girl. It's because he isn't going to hang around afterward.

6) Players are notoriously flakey and have elusive behavior. You'll know why if you hang around a player; they're like call centers. Normal guys who like a girl will make time for the girl, so it's easy to arrange dates and see them whenever you see fit. Players are hard to reach because they're either juggling many girls or have other important things to do. I once went on holiday with one of the biggest players I know, and he was always on the phone setting up dates for when he got back. He even received a text while on holiday that read, "Jason, I want you tonight!" Not sure how much that girl liked him, but we were out meeting other girls that very same night.

7) They are surrounded by a lot of women, female friends as well as other girls they're working on. A player won't be parading a female entourage around when he's chasing after a girl, but I've noticed something about many women. When a guy has other women around him, even if they're just friends, it's easier for the guy to meet new women than if he is just with men. That might seem counter-intuitive

because it means competition for the girl, but it also means the guy's been pre-selected, that there's something attractive about him, and it certainly reduces the risk that the guy's a weirdo or a major loser. The attraction in this case, just like preference for confident males, is also a double-edged sword.

So how's a girl supposed to handle a player? How's a girl even supposed to know she's dealing with a player? What's a girl supposed to do if a lot of the most interesting guys out there are playing around? I've had lots of female friends ask me these questions.

The solution to the problem is actually really simple, so don't sit there over thinking.

Just being with the guy has zero meaning. You have to get the guy to explicitly agree that you are boyfriend and girlfriend, and won't be seeing anyone else. Tell the guy you're seeing you won't have sex with him or anymore sex with him unless he's going to have a monogamous relationship with you, and he'll either stay or run. In fact, mention the word "relationship" and every player for a five mile radius around you will make a run for the hills.

Now, this is not something you say on a first date, hell that'll even scare off a decent guy. It's something you say if you're not sure about a guy, and he's pushing you to have sex, or you've had sex and he keeps calling you for more, but makes no further commitment. I guarantee if a guy genuinely likes you, he'll have no problems starting a relationship, and you get what you want. A player will come up with an excuse not to start a relationship.

He'll probably say, "I like you a lot, but I'm not ready for a relationship yet," or "I think we should slow down a little and just enjoy the moment." But that's just bullshit to get you to change your mind.

It's almost funny sometimes when I tell this to girls who are used to dating players. They tend to look shocked at this very alien concept and say "What? Ask the guy to be in a relationship? But what if I scare him off?"

Ladies and gentlemen, we now live in a world where a lot of women feel pressured and scared to ask a guy to have a relationship. It's a player's heaven!

Players are actually easy to handle and easy to spot; lots of girls just fall for players because they are afraid to scare off a guy they're attracted to. Attraction does funny things to a person's mind. If you can play around with a guy and not get emotionally attached, then go for it. But if you keep getting hurt and hate getting played, then just ask about commitment before having sex with the guy for the first time. At the end of the day, women get to pick.

Chapter 4

I Have No Shame

A lot of women tell men to just be themselves when they approach women, yet a lot of men try to put on an act. You want to know why?

Being ourselves doesn't work!

Most guys are boring to talk to or do things that turn women off. Women might be able to put up with some of the things that men are into once they are in a relationship, but at the beginning? Yeah, right.

No woman is going to enjoy a first date where a guy has little to say, or he talks about subjects she's not into. She won't enjoy a first date where a guy is watching basketball on ESPN while sipping a cold beer, and belching like a caveman.

Men have to impress women to get them interested. It's just how it works. Even the nice guys out there will be doing their best to impress the girls they like. But assholes are different; they will use all sorts of mind games to get what they want, and you'll be surprised at some of the stuff that actually works.

Just off the top of my head I can think of four situations where women are more likely than usual to feel attracted to a man. That doesn't mean a woman will definitely go for a guy, it just means the chances becomes higher than normal.

1) On holiday (a girl's having fun)
2) At a friend's wedding (it's romantic)
3) When a woman sees a man who's good with kids
4) When a woman sees a man who's good with dogs and other cute pets

If you think about it, they've actually made romantic comedies based on all these situations; the movie *Wedding Crashers* is a good example.

I already tried hitting on women under the first two scenarios, but a while back I got the chance to try out tactic number four. One of my best friends, Miranda, bought a dog, a Shiba Inu. It's a Japanese breed, and they're really cute and very friendly.

Soon after buying the dog Miranda had to go on holiday, so while her dog was still a puppy I took care of it for two weeks. I fed it, trained it, and even tried to potty train it and got dog shit all over my hands. Then I decided to take advantage of the situation, so I took some pictures of this cute puppy, shot a video of me trying to train her and put it up on Facebook.

Within twenty-four hours I was flooded with messages and calls from girls asking to see this dog, asking me out for drinks or dinner. I was shocked! It worked even better than my wildest dreams.

When Miranda came back from holiday I told her what I did and asked her why it worked, and she told me it was because I was a big, stocky guy. If I was some skinny dude wearing tight leather pants all the time, girls probably would have thought I was gay. But put a stocky guy together with a cute puppy and it comes off as sweet. Of course after telling me why she said, "You asshole! Now stop pimping my dog out to get girls!"

It's going to be embarrassing when I end up in hell. Satan's going to give me a funny look and say, "You sick bastard, you really tried to pimp out your best friend's cute little puppy for girls?" Unfortunately, yes I did, and it's not that the girls were dumb for falling for my trick. It's just that they didn't understand how low an asshole will stoop just to get a girl interested. I don't think they realize how manipulative we can get.

The most manipulative guys out there will show their sensitive side, will share their personal secrets, and will make a girl feel like he's really opened up to her. But that still won't change the fact that the guy's an asshole.

The Hot and Cold

Assholes will use games to get a girl interested, and then, because they don't want to make a proper commitment to a girl, they'll pull away. This is why a lot of girls complain about men doing the hot and cold or giving mixed signals. One day the guy seems all sweet, the next day he seems indifferent, not calling, and you end up hoping he'll give you a call.

My friend Carol came to me one day for relationship advice, because she was seeing a guy who was doing this hot and cold thing. She met the guy through a friend, and one night they all went out clubbing together. After a few drinks she found herself on the dance floor with the guy. They danced and made out, and then the guy offered to take her back to her place. Obviously she wouldn't have been asking for relationship advice if she just went home to sleep. The two of them had sex and then it all started going really wrong.

They went on dates, and the guy would be really sweet. But then there would be long periods where the guy wouldn't call her, and she didn't know what to do. She didn't want to come off as clingy, but at the same time she couldn't stand not knowing where she stood.

The real warning sign was when she bumped into the guy at a restaurant. He was wearing a suit and was with two other men in suits, so he was obviously at some work function or doing business. But the guy totally blanked her, and there was no way he could have missed her. At first she was mad, and then she started making excuses for the guy. She told herself maybe he didn't see her, or he was doing business and it wouldn't have been appropriate for him to wave at her.

But I can tell you that any guy who really liked a girl for real would have at least smiled and waved before getting back to business.

To make matters worse, the guy just kept lingering. He kept doing the hot and cold, calling her and then backing off, and giving her hope. That's when she came to me for advice. As her friend all I could do was tell her the truth; she might not have wanted to hear it, but the truth was the guy wasn't interested.

Assholes lie, and it hurts to think the guy's not interested, so a woman who likes a guy will want to buy the lie. Whenever you fall for a guy but he's not treating you right, never assume he's the exception and is different from any other asshole, never create excuses to justify why the guy isn't treating you right. The hot and cold is the clearest indication you're dating an asshole.

Remember, next time you're with a guy doing the hot and cold, or you see a big, stocky guy with a cute puppy, stay the hell away!

Chapter 5

Chemistry Is Overrated

Having good chemistry and a spark is always a good start to a relationship. But just because you feel chemistry between you and a guy doesn't mean it's genuine, and doesn't mean you should throw caution to the wind.

Forget pick-up lines. Pick-up lines are for idiots that scare girls off. Men who are really good at playing games put a lot of effort into artificially creating the feeling of a connection. Probably the most important thing an asshole will focus on doing is making a woman feel comfortable to be with him. The guy feels little besides a physical attraction while the girl feels an intense connection. The guy's aim of spending a lot of time on building comfort and connection is so that a girl will lower her guard, think he is nice, and will feel more attracted to him.

When I asked men and women whether they thought chemistry can be artificially engineered, women would consistently say no, and a lot more men would say yes. This is probably why many women seriously underestimate assholes with the wrong intentions. Most women think assholes don't listen, lack the ability to show empathy, and are selfish, and inconsiderate. They're right, but assholes do that *after* they've gotten you emotionally attached and they start to back off.

If you're honest with yourself, you will find that every jerk you have dated in the past somehow managed to attract you at the beginning. There was something sweet about the guy, or something that made you think about him, that made your toes curl. Those feelings weren't a product of just physical attraction; the guy spent time to make you comfortable being with him.

To assume that you can only feel a connection with a nice person is a big underestimation of insincere men. At the beginning deceptive men put in even more effort than average men to get to know a woman. They take every opportunity to say all the right things and do all the right things.

How do jerks know the right things to do? Well, they watch movies, read men's and women's magazines, and books and learn from the people around them. Assholes that chase women a lot know the types of things that are looked upon positively by most women and then model their behaviors after what works.

For example, I've got a female friend that told me she liked generous men who were gentlemen. When I asked her what her definition of a generous gentleman was, she told me he wasn't cheap, was willing to offer to pay for the first date, opened doors for her, and drove her home at the end of the night.

I told her right then and there she needed to add more to her filter, because any asshole with half a brain knows he has to act like that at the start. Her requirements were basically only good for filtering out lazy idiots who didn't understand dating etiquette.

Knowing what to say is a bit harder, but it's still not hard for a well practiced man. Assholes that say all the right things can do it because the woman tells them what to say. In other words the woman tells the guy what she likes, and he catches on.

Normally when people first meet, they try and find out as much about each other as possible, so an asshole has the opportunity to ask a woman many leading and probing questions without coming off as strange. Smart sales people essentially do the same thing; they ask their customers what their needs are and then try to cater to the needs.

Let me use the example of interests. A woman is on a date, and the man asks what her hobbies are. She says she likes to do yoga; she's been doing it for eight years now and is considering teaching some day. He immediately thinks of all the things he knows about yoga or connected to yoga, smiles and says:

"Wow, that's so cool! It must have taken a lot of hard work to get to your level. I do yoga at my gym as well, but I'm just a beginner. In fact I have a problem with a few moves. Maybe you should give me a couple of lessons, for free of course! Ha ha"

What he's done here is:

1) Shown interest in her passion
2) Shown empathy
3) Praised her
4) Talked about her and himself, thus showing a degree of connection
5) Made an attempt at a silly joke and smiled as well.
6) Changed his voice tone throughout to show genuine interest because voice tonality and body language often convey more meaning than what's actually being said.

This is just a short transcript, and you might read that and think you wouldn't fall for that. You're right, you wouldn't. But that's because you're not attracted to the guy in this hypothetical conversation.

If a woman is attracted to a man and the man shows empathy and genuine interest, then it can amplify the feelings of attraction.

By having a broad range of knowledge and experiences, a smart guy can have a lot of topics to talk about in order to quickly build feelings of emotional and intellectual chemistry. He just needs to show a keen interest in a woman and listen to the things that she has to say. This is especially easy if the guy has a good understanding of psychology and had a lot of chances to practice what works and what doesn't. If a guy is meeting people daily, and each time he's analyzing social interactions, it doesn't take long to figure out what people like.

Don't put too much importance on initial chemistry. You might need chemistry to start dating, but having chemistry doesn't mean you've landed yourself Prince Charming. A lot of players are very manipulative and are really good actors; their strategies are geared specifically to building rapport. It takes time to get to know someone, so don't throw caution to the wind or you'll miss out on any red flag behaviors.

Chapter 6

Don't Go Gaga

Older women tend to be better with men than younger women. Older women are also generally less likely to be played by men than younger women, and the reason is that they've been there and done that. They have more experience with men and tend to exercise more self-control when it comes to interacting with men.

Self-control is a hard thing to practice. But you need a level of self-control if you want a man to love you, or if you want to avoid assholes.

Think of two forces acting on you when you're attracted to someone. On the one hand there's the instinctive primal side, the side that drives love and lust and gives you the butterflies in your stomach feeling. Then there's the logical, rational side, where you consciously decide what to do. Sometimes these sides come into conflict.

It's very similar to eating and dieting. Say you want to go on a diet. You have your instinctive side that drives you to want to eat even though you want to lose weight, and then there's your conscious side telling yourself not to eat. You can pretty much feel the conflict between the two sides when dieting.

When it comes to dating men, you can't just do whatever you feel like. You can't go for someone just because you're attracted. It's no different from pigging out every day with zero self-control; it's not going to get you the best results. It doesn't mean you can't enjoy yourself on a date, but at the back of your mind, your logical mind has to be able to override that primal side and see through the man's confidence or humor or charm and notice if the guy has good values and integrity.

Even I'm careful when I go on a date. Or rather, when I used to go dating, since soon there'll be no women dating me. When I go on a date, no matter how hot the girl is, my logical side is always ticking. In fact the hotter she is, the more careful I am, because I don't want to get my heart broken (yeah, some women play men too). In the back of my mind in addition to enjoying myself and having a good time, I'm always asking myself a few key questions:

"Is she genuinely a nice person? Does she treat the people around her well? Does she love her family? Is she nice? IS SHE NICE?"

or

"Oh look she's cheating on her boyfriend with me. Will she rip my heart out in future too? WILL SHE RIP MY HEART OUT IN THE FUTURE?

and

"Oh look, I just paid for the movie, dinner, and now drinks. Does she expect me to pay for all this shit for the rest of the time we're together? Is she a gold digger? Is she a gold digger? IS SHE A GOLD DIGGER?!"

this one's good

"This girl's been acting weird all night. Is she a psycho? Will she cut my dick off when she's mad? WILL SHE CUT MY DICK OFF AND FLUSH IT DOWN THE TOILET IF SHE'S MAD?!"

and I guess the most important one

"Am I lying to myself because I want pussy? Am I lying to myself because I want pussy? AM I LYING TO MYSELF BECAUSE I WANT PUSSY?"

Well as you can see, since you're a woman the key questions you'll be asking yourself will be very different from the ones I routinely ask myself. My point is simply that if even an asshole such as myself is careful on dates, then a girl certainly should exercise some self-control and not get carried away on a date with an attractive guy.

I know it's hard to leave a guy if you've been with him for a long time and are emotionally attached to him, but it's not hard to leave a guy when you're still getting to know him.

The problem with dating these days is that so many people are so focused about feelings that they forget dating is also about getting to know someone else and discovering character. Dating is about finding out whether the man (or woman) has integrity.

Chapter 7

The Biggest Mistakes Women Make

Women might want to avoid players, but there are guys out there that are a lot worse than the average player. Take me, for example. When a guy is dumb enough and selfish enough, he'll destroy everything that's good in his life, everything he's ever cared about, before he realizes what he's done. But the real tragedy isn't the dumbass that loses everything; he deserves his lot in life. The tragedy is all the collateral damage that he does, all the people he hurts because of his selfish ways.

I once dated a really nice girl, we lived together. She kept our place clean, she took care of me when I was sick, she stuck with me when I wasn't doing well in my career, she was beautiful, and above all she loved me and thought I was her soul mate. But I took her for granted for seven years; I even cheated on her. For seven years she loved me and waited for me, hoping I'd change and spend the rest of my life with her. In the end she left me because she knew there would be no future.

Thankfully she's now with a guy who loves her and treats her well. But that doesn't change the fact that she spent seven years dating an asshole, a dumbass that didn't give her the love that she deserved and hurt her in the process.

I'll probably go to hell for what I've done, but I'm not dead yet, so before that happens I'm going to explain why sometimes good girls end up with guys like myself, so that you or your friends don't have to make the same mistakes.

Mistake 1: Having Sex Too Soon

Ok, first of all let's get this straight. I am not a pastor or a priest, preaching how people should only have sex after marriage. You should have the freedom to do whatever you like; in fact you could run down the block totally naked, and I wouldn't give a shit. I'd probably be taking pictures but I wouldn't give a shit.

Waiting on sex is not just about filtering out players. The problem with sex for a woman is that it has the potential to get a woman emotionally attached to the guy. That isn't a bad thing if she's with a decent guy, in fact it's the most wonderful thing in the world, but if the man happens to be an asshole then she's going to be screwed (pun intended).

To understand this more, you've got to understand a little biology. Men might want sex all the time, but sex has a bigger effect on women than on men. When a woman has sex, especially if it's good sex with orgasms involved, her brain will release a hormone called oxytocin, and this hormone will do two things.

It has the potential to get a woman emotionally attached to the guy she's having sex with, with the probability increasing the more times she has sex with the man, and it has the effect of distorting and disrupting sound judgment.

Oxytocin basically acts like a drug, but instead of being addicted to a drug, a woman can become addicted to a man. Oxytocin is the reason some women stick with their cheating, abusive, lying, inconsiderate, loser boyfriends or husbands. Even if it's clear to all her friends that the guy she's with is a gigantic prick, she'll find it too painful to leave the guy. It's not because she's crazy or weak; it's because oxytocin is at work.

So don't have sex with a guy too soon. If you get emotionally attached before you find out he's an asshole then you'll be hurting badly later on.

Mistake 2: Over-romanticizing

You know why a lot more women watch chick flicks than men? It appeals to a woman's natural desires and senses. It's the same reason women are more likely than men to cry at a friend's wedding. Women desire a beautiful romance with a man who'll rock their world, a Prince Charming so to speak. Sure, women these days don't need a man, but the desire for that romance is there never the less.

There's nothing wrong with romance. But over-romanticizing is a huge problem because the women will start to deviate from reality, and every time they start liking someone, they'll start giving that person more credit than the person deserves.

Read this and take note: *A lot of women fall in love with a fantasy of a man, more than with the man who's actually in front of them*

When a woman does that, an asshole can easily take advantage, because as soon as she becomes attracted to a man she'll start to put him on a pedestal and will fail to see any danger signals. She'll start to see things happening in the way she wants it to happen, rather than seeing the reality of the situation.

Mistake 3: Hoping Things Will Get Better

Hope is a good thing in a time of crisis. But when it comes to men, hope is the worst possible thing you can have. The reason is because if a relationship is healthy and everything is good, then there's no need to hope. A woman only starts hoping when something is seriously wrong with the relationship or with the guy. Just look at my ex and myself, it's like a big cautionary tale.

Assholes love it when women hope; otherwise they wouldn't be able to string women along. As I mentioned earlier, every time a guy starts hitting on you, he's doing his best to impress you. It's only after some time that an asshole will revert back to his baseline personality, which is basically his normal personality and how he normally treats women, and that's when an asshole needs to make excuses to justify his behavior. That's when he starts to feed on hope.

A female friend once asked me, "Why can't men just be honest and tell women they're looking to play?" Well, assholes might treat women badly, but they're not stupid. They're not going to walk around wearing a sign with flashing neon lights advertising that they're assholes. No asshole is ever going to come up to you and say, "Hi, I'm Fred, I want to have sex with you and then I'm going to run for my life!"

What you get at the beginning isn't what you'll always get later, and then you either accept the guy for who he is or walk away. I do know women who married assholes knowing exactly what they were getting themselves into, but those women weighed the pros and the cons and made a decision. I know one woman who married a man who was fun to be with and made her laugh all the time, she also knew he would cheat on her constantly. She married him anyway because she didn't want to spend her life with a faithful but boring man.

I don't want you to read all this and think things are hopeless. If you're with a jerk it just means the current guy's not the one. You can always find happiness. You just need to dump that asshole to free yourself up and find a better man.

Mistake 4: Thinking a Man Will Change

I never really understood why women want to change men. Why would you find an interesting bad boy that's running wild and free, and turn him into a boring, docile, faithful guy? Why not just find a boring, docile, faithful guy in the first place? It's a conspiracy, I tell you, an evil plot to enslave mankind. You women just want to turn us into your slaves!

Actually, I know why some women try to change men. They find a guy they're interested in, and he's got a lot of attractive qualities, but then it turns out he's also messed up, or a selfish prick, and no one's perfect. The woman doesn't want to leave the guy because she likes him, so she tries to eliminate the bad things about the man, tries to "fix" the guy.

The problem is that few men are capable of changing, even if they wanted to. Men are like the scorpion in the fable about the scorpion and the frog.

One day a frog was swimming down a stream when he comes across a scorpion. The scorpion, wishing to cross the stream asked the frog to carry it to the other side. When the frog asked the scorpion how he could be sure that the scorpion won't sting him, the scorpion replied that if he did then they would both drown. The frog thought about this for a moment and agreed to carry the scorpion on his back across the stream. Before they reach the other side however, the frog felt a sudden pain in his back and realizes that the scorpion has stung him. "Why did you sting me, Mr. Scorpion?" the frog gasped, "Now we shall both die!" The scorpion replied, "I could not help myself, it is in my nature." Then they both sank into the waters of the swift flowing stream.

Tell me, ladies, if you saw some drug dealers on the corner of some street, do you go up to them and tell them drugs are bad for them? No, you stay away from them!

If some creepy looking homeless guy followed you down the street in the dark for five minutes, do you turn around and tell him to get a job? No, you kick him in the nuts and then you run!

If you wake up in the middle of the night to find some guy carrying your TV out your backdoor, do you bother telling him that stealing is wrong? No, you shoot him in the leg and tell the cops it was self defense!

Yet for some reason when it comes to jerks, some women will sit there for years hoping the guys will change.

You can't change animal nature. You can't change a selfish prick if he's been a selfish prick all his life. Think of it in terms of alcoholics. Alcoholics find it hard to stay sober even when they know their drinking problem is ruining their own lives, and hurting their loved ones. Assholes are very similar, and the only difference between the two groups is there is a twelve-step program for recovering alcoholics, whereas assholes need a fifty-six step program.

For an asshole to truly change and for that change to be permanent, he has to want to change for himself. The few assholes that do change usually change in between relationships, when they're lying in bed one night and come to the realization the way they've lived their lives is wrong. This has nothing to do with love or a woman, because people generally don't change for other people, they change for themselves.

Women love to hear stories of men changing for women, because one of the most romantic ideals out there is that if a man loved a woman enough, and if she's special enough, he will change for her. You see it in chick flicks all the time: some messed-up guy is seriously flawed in some way, meets the female protagonist, falls in love, and changes to become a better man. Most women associate themselves with the special girl who changes the guy at the end, but never with the dozens of women the guy hurt in the past.

So it's no surprise whenever I discuss this point with female friends there will always be a few that say they have seen men change. They see a guy who was formerly a total prick, and the biggest player meets their friend, treats her well, settles down, and marries her.

But what most girls see and remember are usually the good years, and not what happens when the jerk eventually changes back to his true self. Most assholes will eventually get married, and that's because they think marriage and kids are part of a natural process in life. A player I know once told me he'd given up finding the woman of his dreams. Instead he was just going to find the mother of his children. I truly feel sorry for his future wife if that's how he feels, because she's going to be marrying a guy who only loves himself and not her. People will go to their wedding and remember the fairy tale, but not all the crap that will occur years later.

Don't hate me for revealing what men are really like and discussing reality. I did say I was going to tell the truth and not sugar coat it. But I'll say it again: there are good, interesting men out there. You can find your Prince Charming. Just don't expect an asshole to turn into him.

Chapter 8

Freaking Out about Commitment

As my friend Sarah put it, "We're sick of hooking up with men and being in relationships that go nowhere"

So what's up with men these days? Why are so many unwilling to make a commitment to a woman, especially when it comes to marriage? Why do men marry later and later these days?

The reason men are different from our grandparents' era is because back then all men were expected to get married; there was pressure from society. Also, far fewer women had sex before marriage, which meant there was a much smaller market for players. Nowadays men can pick whatever lifestyle suits them, and that means there will be players that play till their dicks drop off.

These days a lot of guys don't understand what responsibility means. Responsibility to a player sounds more like a shriek or the death knell announcing the end of his manhood. We now live in a culture where men can get away with playing around, so girls like Sarah will lose out.

Different guys have different reasons for not settling down. In fact there are so many reasons I can't list them all. Some just want to play around, and others come from broken families and don't have a healthy example when it comes to relationships.

For me, I think it's always been a bit of both. My parents got divorced when I was only two; my biological father cheated on my mum, and I've never seen him since. When I was a kid, I always thought I'll get married some-day, but when I grew up every time I thought about marriage, I would always come up with really negative reasons not to get married. Here are some of them, and I don't deny that I'm fucked up (please don't hate me):

1) **Loss of Freedom**. When you date, it's all about having fun and having feelings. But when it comes to marriage, you'd better be sure you can see yourself with that other person for the rest of your life. Yes! The rest of your frigging life! You need to see that person every day till death do you part! Sure, you can always speed it up by killing the asshole or the bitch and some people do. But those people are in jail and you never get to meet them.

2) **Sex**. The longer you date someone, the worse the sex tends to get. Let's use the example of blow-jobs. When a guy first starts dating a girl, the blowjobs are often so good the guy feels like he's getting attacked by a high-powered vacuum cleaner. Years later, what happens? The girl who used to risk lockjaw just to give the guy a good time now gives him three licks and a pat on the back. Now, you girls might think it's terrible to complain about the shitty blowjobs, but it's even worse for you! Whilst some guy used to take the effort to get you in the mood, go down on you till your leg started twitching, and you used to scream so loud the neighbors had to call the police. Years later all you've got is some lazy, fat asshole lying on top of you and the only thing you really want to say to him isn't "Baby, I love you," but "Are you done yet?"

3) **Boredom**. Over time things might get really, really boring. Now, I use the word "might" because some couples actually

36

make the effort to keep each other happy. But a lot of people will get sick of each other after five to ten years. It's not a surprise because for some reason people get lazy and boring. Picnics and public fornication are replaced by conversations about the baby-sitter, the kid's grades, and the weather. There is a solution to all this: pick someone with a great sense of humor. I'm serious. If you've got someone with a sense of humor and they crack you up everyday then be grateful.

4) **Tits and Ass**. When a guy is single, staring at tits and ass is a pleasure, and chasing after them is fun. After marriage T&A becomes a dangerous temptation.

5) **Money**. When you're single you're financially independent. Once you're married, you can't even make big expenditures without explaining why. Just make sure to marry someone who earns more, so you can profit if there's a divorce.

6) **Annoying Habits**. You don't really know someone till you've really lived with them. Seeing someone a few times a week is totally different from having to sleep next to that person and seeing them in their natural habitat daily. For example here are some of the things that might lead to divorce or murder:

    *   Your husband leaves the toilet seat up all the time. Your wife bitches about the toilet seat being left up all the time.
    *   Your partner snores like a fucking barn animal, which was bearable or even cute the first time you had sex but after a while you just want to put a pillow over the person's head and suffocate them.
    *   You're about to drift off to sleep and have to work early in the morning when all of a sudden and totally unprovoked the other person lets out a big fart in your bed! Then you have to spend the rest of the night wondering if it's better to let the noxious gases out or keep it under the covers.

Okay, I'm not about to kill my future wife, I was just kidding. But you get the general idea, I'm pretty messed up and that's why I'm still single, and the sad thing is I'm not alone. Lots of assholes will actually worry about the same points I brought up, and it's funny, you actually want to marry us?

But that's why you need to avoid guys like myself. There are assholes that are a lot worse than players, because they date women but never settle down, and that wastes a huge amount of a woman's time, not to mention the heartbreak that follows. So every girl should learn to spot early on whether a guy's going to end up wasting her time.

Chapter 9

How to Tell if a Guy's Wasting Your Time

Lots of girls have told me they're not looking for marriage when they meet a guy. So what's my concern with marriage? You might not be thinking about marriage when you start dating a guy, but you don't want to find out after seven years that the prick you're dating is still not ready to settle down, like my ex did. What happens if you break up then? You've wasted years waiting for a guy when there wasn't going to be any future, and that time could have been spent looking for the right guy.

There are two main reasons men get married, either they meet a special girl and fall in love, or it's about timing, they hit a certain age and consciously decide they should settle down. For most guys it's a combination of the two. Yeah, even the nice guys will sometimes wait because they want to get to a stage in their career where they're financially secure.

But when it comes to guys who fear commitment it's pretty much always the second reason. It doesn't matter how great the girl is, it doesn't matter what you do, the guy will find it impossible to settle down until he starts feeling he's getting old. The following are some of the reasons why an asshole will eventually settle down, but as you will see it's got nothing to do with the woman.

1) **Single Forever = Lonely**. Contrary to what most people think, once you peel away all the womanizing behavior and macho exterior, most players I've met are pretty lonely guys. That might not hit them when they're still young, but it will hit them one day when they start feeling old.

2) **All their friends have gotten married**. Picking up girls might have been fun when girls were into the guy. It won't be fun when the guy's balding, all his friends are married, and he's an old dude using the same pick-up techniques he's been using for twenty years. Remember when you were eighteen, and that dirty old man was hitting on your friends? That guy used to be a good-looking player! Now it just comes off as sad.

3) **Someone to take care of them**. Again, it's cool to be single when the guy's body was firm and he was able to bench press two hundred pounds. But what happens when a guy gets old? What's a guy supposed to do if he needs to take a shit, and on he's on his way to the toilet, he trips and breaks a hip? Is he going to call his old flames Stacey and Michelle, who by the way got married thirty years ago? Or is he going to rely on his wife?

4) **Kids**. Although the concept is scary for some people, and some kids are so annoying you just want to kick them in the side of the head and tell them to shut the fuck up, with your own kids, it's something different. A guy once told me you don't know what love really is till you've had your own kids. Even assholes will want kids. If assholes didn't breed, then assholes would go extinct.

Yes, assholes think differently. You might want a big white wedding, but don't assume everyone thinks the same way. If a guy doesn't ever want to get married then that's his call, but if you want to get married, you need to make sure the guy's going to be on the same page. Here are some early warning signals that the guy isn't ready.

1) He finds excuses not to commit to a relationship with you. Just about all players fear commitment, and the greater the level of commitment, the bigger the fear. If you find out a guy is a player, then the chances of him considering marriage later on is going to be much lower than the average guy.

2) No faith in marriage. If a guy is constantly joking about the negatives of marriage (like I just did) then that's an indicator. Some guys will even explicitly say they don't believe in marriage.

3) You never get to see his parents. Unless a guy's parents are psychopaths, a guy will always bring the girl he loves to see his parents.

4) He has problems showing public affection. Many guys are shy about showing public affection, but if a guy never holds your hand in public, never allows you to put your head on his shoulder, and walks in front of instead of next to you, then he doesn't want to give other women indications that he's exclusive with you.

5) He is scared to say I love you. In addition, he often thinks things are moving too fast.

6) Doesn't want to talk about the future. People should date for fun and not worry about the future, and you shouldn't talk about the future till you've been together a long while. But a guy who fears commitment will freak out and change the subject every time the future is brought up, and when you do finally talk about it he'll find reasons not to commit.

Examples:

I'm not ready to settle down (he's telling the truth!)

I'm don't really know what I want

I don't think you understand me well enough. (Then you spend years trying to understand him)

He starts telling you to change certain aspects of your personality like it's a major deal breaker, but doesn't break up with you either.

No Congruence between Words and Behavior

The one thing that is common to all assholes is the lack of congruence between words and behavior.

Most assholes:

Say the right things ("I like you," and "you're so special to me") and do the wrong things (treat you like crap)

Guys who fear commitment often do the opposite:

They might do all the right things (treat you well) but will tell you in your face all the wrong things ("I don't want to settle down")

Just as it is with players, the solution to the problem is a lot less complex than most women think. If a guy keeps dragging it on, *you just need to ask the man if he will marry you*, and then of course you need to hear what the guy is saying and not what you want to hear. A lot of women never force their men to give them a definitive answer because the relationship is steady and they don't want to rock the boat. But I'll tell you this: if a man was truly in love and didn't want to lose his woman, marriage is not a barrier.

I know one woman who never forced her man to give her an answer, so she ended up dating the guy for fourteen years, from when she was twenty till she was thirty-four. Finally she had enough and wanted a definitive answer from the man, and when she was thirty-four, they broke up because he still wouldn't marry her. I guess it would be fine if she was okay with dating a guy for fourteen years. But she wasn't, she was bitter and torn inside for having wasted fourteen years on the guy. She could have asked after, say, four years and saved herself a decade of waiting, but she didn't want to rock the boat.

When it comes to men don't assume anything. Getting a definitive answer from a man is probably one of the few times in life where it's better to have the shit hit the fan earlier rather than later.

So ask! Just be frank and honest and tell a guy that if he still wants to be with you then he needs to make a commitment. You don't want to start water boarding the guy, or use other forms of interrogation techniques, and it's crazy to ask when you're only a few months into the relationship. But you'll be surprised; usually the truth is staring you in the face. A lot of women over-think only because they don't want to accept the truth, which is that the guy they're with is an asshole.

Don't hope, don't try to change him, don't try to change his mind, and don't wonder if there's something you could have done better. If he loves you, he'll make a commitment; if he's messed up in the head like I am, then you could be the most amazing women in the world with *Superwoman* tattooed on your ass, and the guy will still never settle down.

A word of warning about the *crying game:*

It's hard enough to break up with a guy you have feelings for. But a lot of assholes make it even harder by using what I call the crying game. When you dump a guy, don't be surprised if he apologizes, breaks down, and even starts crying, begging for you to come back. Don't be surprised if he keeps calling you, even though you want to shut him out.

He's not doing this because he loves you. He's doing this because he's scared to be alone. When he does this, be strong. Don't take the guy back; if you forgive him once, he'll do it again, and before you know it you've wasted seven years on him. What you should do is tell him to stop crying, stop being a little bitch, and learn to treat women right.

Chapter 10

The Really Mean Bastards

Believe it or not, I'm actually still friends with all my ex-girlfriends. I may have been a bad boyfriend, but for some reason some of them still hang out with me. I'm not trying to excuse my behavior, I'm still an asshole, but I think they still talk to me because I was never a mean bastard to them. I may have done some pretty bad things in my lifetime, but there are guys out there that are a lot worse than me.

As part of the research for this book, I talked to hundreds of girls to get their perspectives on relationships, and to hear about their experiences, so I've heard some really bad horror stories. There might be players and selfish pricks out there, but when you start hearing stories of the biggest narcissists and abusive guys, that's something else altogether.

The worst thing is when I find out a female friend is still dating one of these guys. A long time ago, this one guy pinned my friend down during an argument and almost strangled her. She had to escape from their apartment and stay over at a friend's place just to be safe.

Later that night when the girl called me, she was still crying and was emotionally distressed. I told her she should consider calling the cops on the guy, but instead what happened? A few weeks later, I bumped into them walking down the street together like nothing had happened. Apparently when she tried to dump him, he started crying and begging her not to leave him; he told her how much he loved her and then went out and bought her a ring. She thought he was sincere and forgave him.

It's just so frustrating seeing things like that. It makes me want to sit myself down and then bang my head repeatedly against a table or something. The scary thing is that once I asked around, I realized many women have been abused emotionally or physically by their men, and these were just the girls who shared the truth. I'm sure most women keep their secrets to themselves.

In the good old days families used to have to approve of a guy before a girl could even start seeing the guy, let alone marry him. I realize now why things were done that way: it was to protect the girl in case the guy she brought home turned out to be a freak. Man if I was a dad and my daughter brought back one of these guys, I would chase the bastard off my property with an axe or a sawed off shotgun.

I hate to think such men even exist, but they do so I'm going to explain how to spot some of these guys. So ladies and gentlemen, it is not my pleasure to bring to you the fucking circus freak show.

Freak 1: The Narcissist

Narcissists are people who love only themselves, and even when they are doing nice things for other people, the ultimate aim is to benefit themselves. When it's no longer in their own interest to be with someone, they will dump that person and start a relationship with someone else relatively quickly.

A narcissistic guy will think of himself as normal, and he'll probably be looking for a girlfriend just like anyone else. The problem is narcissists suffer from delusions of grandeur, and the guy will expect a woman to fulfill all of his desires no matter how extreme or selfish they are. Just about every woman the guy meets won't be good enough, which is why narcissists tend to serial date.

I know girls who have dated narcissists, and they had to jump through fire hoops to please these men, only to be treated like crap in return. It's not cool; it's like watching someone getting the life sucked out of them.

The girls stay with these guys because narcissists are extremely manipulative. They can be very sweet at times, and know how to make a girl feel like it's her fault that he's not happy, so she tries even harder to please him.

Narcissists are not easy to spot at the beginning unless you're aware of what to look for, because when they first approach a girl, they can be very charming and charismatic, so the girl won't be aware that she's interacting with a selfish prick.

The following are early signs that a guy's a narcissist.

1) Look at the way they treat other people. They're often rude to those around them and shows no appreciation or empathy, from cab drivers to waiters, and even to their parents in extreme cases. Basically the guy's an asshole in general, but when he's chasing after a girl, he's going to treat her very well; it's only later when he knows she's attracted to him that he starts treating her like everyone else.
2) Narcissists are often cocky and boastful. You'll also find they think they're always in the right about everything.
3) They take offense easily if someone doesn't think they're some sort of superstar. If you say something that puts them down, even if it's meant to be a joke, they'll get pissed off.

4) Another way to spot narcissists is by finding out how their previous relationships went. After all, they hop from girl to girl relatively quickly. Now, you can't ask them outright so the best way to do it is to feed their ego slightly. Just ask questions like, "So why is a great guy like you single? Why did your previous relationships not work out?" These guys have big egos, so if you feed their narcissism, they often start blabbering on about how crap all their previous girlfriends have been, and any guy who has only bad things to say about all his ex-girlfriends is usually an asshole.

5) Have you seen a narcissist do something really selfish, and he's treating other people or yourself like crap, and you're thinking, "That's not him," or "He's acting out of character" because he's shown you his sweet side? Hell no! That *is his character*. He's acting out of character when he's being nice; open your eyes and see it!

Freak 2: The Abusive Guy

People are often confused as to why any woman would put up with abuse and doesn't just walk away. But abusive relationships never start off that way. In the beginning the guy always acts very sweet. If the guy was abusive at the start then of course the girl would be alerted and dump him.

Women who can see through a player's game can still fall for an abusive guy because the abusive guy doesn't necessarily want sex, he wants control. He may act differently from other jerks at the beginning and he could seem like he's really in love with the girl.

There are two types of abuse, emotional and physical. Physical abuse is easy to spot because the bruises are visible, but most abusive men are also emotionally abusive. An emotionally abusive man is often manipulative and skilled in pushing the blame, to make the girl feel like she's not good enough or that everything is her fault. That's why many girls hold on to abusive men. The guy will slowly break down a girl's self-esteem, and she will feel like it's her fault that he's become this way.

After abusing the girl, whether physically or psychologically the abusive guy will often apologize, say he loves her, and promise to change so the girl forgives him and doesn't leave. He might even use the crying game, and that's because despite acting tough on the outside, he's actually got self-esteem issues himself.

When the girl takes the guy back, he will gain control, and the more times the girl takes the guy back, the more control he will gain as her self-esteem is slowly lowered. The important thing to remember about abusive men is:

They will always be abusive no matter what their promises are.

Most abusive men have been abused themselves or have witnessed their mothers getting abused as a child, and thus they have a very unhealthy perception of relationships. The only way they can change is if they admit they have a problem and actually go through long-term therapy. All the crying and promises of change is just one big lie, and they will always go back to their old ways.

Forget everything I've taught you about players and other assholes. These guys are very different and very dangerous, and the early warnings signs are also different.

1) They are really insecure, so when they start liking a girl, they'll try to sweep the girl off her feet and rush the relationship along very quickly. Have you ever found yourself thinking, "What the hell is wrong with this guy? Can't he slow down?" That's the first danger signal.

2) Obviously there have been healthy romances that started very fast. However, if you try and slow the guy down, normal guys will respect that and back off. An abusive guy will start

to act possessive, will not want you to do anything without him, will say things to guilt you into not slowing down, and will keep the relationship going at his pace.

3) He'll start to get jealous and won't like it if you spend time with your family, friends or co-workers, and definitely not with male friends. If he doesn't become your center of attention, he will become angry and accuse you of cheating or flirting with other men without just cause.

4) If you learn he's had a childhood where he was abused or he witnessed his mother being abused, then that might be a warning sign too. Many people have had a troubled childhood, and that by itself isn't a problem. But if you ask a guy about his family, and it comes out he was abused, and he happens to be showing all the other red flags behaviors, then it's probably a good idea to leave the guy.

I don't know what advice to give other than to say, stay away from men who show such red flag behaviors; if you're already dating an abusive guy, dump him and tell him to get help. If you have problems leaving because he won't let you and threatens you, then I'll share another secret about abusive guys.

They like hitting women but they hate having the shit kicked out of them, so forget "live and let live" and go with an "eye for an eye". Get some guy friends to help you out. Once the guy gets drop kicked in the head a few times, he'll learn to behave. In fact, he may not even be able to walk or drive so you know you'll be safe!

Okay I was just kidding. I'm not actually advocating violence. But you should really call the police and possibly get a restraining order, or get some male friends to protect you. This is not something you should handle all on your own.

The Others

Drug addicts, alcoholics, and guys who get in trouble with the law. Basically, all you have to do is think of the most messed up guys on the planet, and for some reason there'll be girls dating them.

The pattern is always the same: The guy starts off showing his good side, he chases after a girl and gets her interested, and then the freak rears its head weeks or months later.

I have no right to judge these guys; I guess a lot of them have had a tough childhood, but that doesn't mean they're not dangerous for a girl. I also can't force a girl to leave a guy no matter how messed up or abusive the guy is to the girl. I guess when it comes to freaks, or assholes in general, the only person who can save a girl is herself.

If you're with a freak, the key is to ask yourself if you are happy. Pretend for one second you were single and giving relationship advice to a friend who had your problems. What advice would you give? Try taking out all the excuses your man makes, all the happy memories, all the comments like "I love you, you mean so much to me." When you strip everything out and you find yourself unhappy, then that's the clearest indication that you need to leave.

Chapter 11

Avoiding Cheaters

I know the chapter title sounds like I'm going to teach you how to spot if a guy's going to cheat in the future, but I can't do that, because even good people can potentially cheat if they're treated badly in a relationship.

What I can say is that *if you pick an asshole then he'll most likely cheat in the future*, whereas a decent guy in a loving relationship won't cheat.

I also can't help you stop your man from cheating. What can you do? Pin a GPS tracking device and a taser to his dick? So if he cheats the son of a bitch gets a nasty shock, starts twitching on the ground, and you find out? Nah, if a guy cheats, all you can do is decide whether or not you're going to leave him.

What I want to address is how to deal with a man if he's cheating on someone else and hitting on you. My friend Melissa asked me the other night about this because it seems like a lot of men who hit on women already have wives or girlfriends, and my friend knows a couple of girls who had put themselves into the position of a mistress.

I know it's pointless to mention the obvious, which is that a woman shouldn't go for a man who's taken already, and that also it's wrong to cheat. But I'm hardly the person who's got the right to judge anyone else. After all, I've cheated, I've lied, and I've even pimped out puppies just to get girls.

What I will do is explain how a cheater operates in enough detail to hopefully ruin the guy's game. (I expect to get punched some day by a player for disclosing all this!)

Here's how a guy plays the game. If a guy's cheating but doesn't disclose he's got a wife or a girlfriend, then treat him like any other potential player. If he wants to have sex with you, you ask him to be in a monogamous relationship before you'll have sex with him.

He'll either run because he's taken and doesn't have the time to do that, or he'll want the relationship (not monogamous by the way) but will have to disclose that he's actually taken already. The reason he has to disclose is because sooner or later you're going to wonder why he's always unavailable. After all, he's got to spend time with his wife or girlfriend. At that point giving him the middle finger becomes an option.

A lot of guys, however, will disclose that they're taken already even before the woman asks. There are two reasons why the guy does this. First of all, it's to put the woman at ease and pretend they're just having a friendly chat, and the guy hopes to create some sort of a connection in those brief moments. It also allows him to throw in a deceptive line:

"My wife doesn't love me anymore," or "Things haven't been working out with my girlfriend and we might break up soon."

The line is the key! By throwing in the line, the guy gives the girl hope he's going to leave his previous partner pretty soon. He also removes a lot of the guilt the girl feels, because after all, if things are bad with his wife or girlfriend already, she's not responsible for breaking them up.

Assholes always use key lines to give a girl hope and string her along. I mentioned one earlier: "*I like you a lot* but I'm not ready for a relationship *yet*" The italicized parts are the deceptive parts used to give a girl hope that things will change. Wording is very important; if it's vague enough, then a girl who's attracted won't notice the lie.

That's why cheaters will frequently say their relationships are not working out. They're trying to find a girl who will believe the lie. But know this: If a guy's cheating on his previous partner, what's stopping him from cheating on you?

Also, when it comes to married men, very few will leave their wives for a mistress. Married men who are cheating are usually just trying to get sex on the side. They're not looking to break up their family or end up in a messy divorce.

Men who are taken already but hitting on you are no different from other players. Sex, lies, and manipulation make up the game. Play the game at your own peril. It might start off as some fun, and you're not looking for a future with the guy, but before long the oxytocin kicks in and then you start to go crazy.

If you don't have enough baggage in your life already and you need more, going after men who are taken already is the fastest way to do it.

Chapter 12

Saying Bye to That Asshole

I almost had a nervous breakdown the other day. It's become unbearable.

You have no idea how hard it is to spend all day thinking about and writing about assholes. Hell, I'm even thinking about assholes whenever I go eat or take a dump. You're probably sharing my pain by now, and I want to move on to the fun stuff and teach you all the things that attract decent men. So I'm going to teach you the best way to get that asshole out of your head and out of your life forever.

The Cruelest Deed

Some time ago, a really good female friend of mine (more like a sister) was dating this guy who turned out to be a piece of trash. We all felt the guy was too immature, but who were we to step in and tell our friend how to live her life?

They had been dating for almost three years when he proposed. Nobody pushed him, and my friend certainly didn't. He came up with the idea all by himself. When all her friends found out, everyone was happy for her.

As a good friend to the girl, I took the time to get to know this guy. I hung out with him, partied with him, and even helped organize his stag party. Everything seemed great; he even called my friend during the weekend we were away for his stag to tell her how much he loved her. Then a week later, out of the blue the guy called me and told me we needed to have a talk.

He told me he had lost feelings for my friend, and not only did he tell me that, he basically told me it was my friend's fault because there were certain things that she did and certain aspects of her personality that he didn't like. I was shocked. I wanted to grab him and kick the shit out of him. But I couldn't because I had to see if I could change his mind.

Nobody could force this guy to love my friend, but if there were things about her that he didn't like then why did he propose? On top of that the selfish prick didn't want to feel guilty, so he justified what he did and tried to make it look like it was my friend's fault that the wedding wouldn't happen.

People were flying in from all over the world to attend this wedding. So because this guy felt it was okay to propose on a whim, and cancel on a whim, my friend not only had to deal with the pain, but she also had to call up everyone on her side one by one and tell them the wedding was cancelled. Can you imagine how bad that feels? For weeks after he backed out, people would go up to her and say, "Heard you're getting married! Congrats!" Then they had to witness the pain on her face.

Things actually got worse.

The guy was living in her place and refused to move out immediately, and my friend being a nice person let him take his time to find a new place. He stayed and lingered for two weeks. For two weeks she had to sleep under the same roof as the man she had thought she was going to marry, the man who had ripped her heart out on a whim.

The guy even had the nerve to act all upbeat like nothing wrong had happened, and he went out to party while staying at her place. Then after he finally moved out, he would call her and wanted to see her. By dragging it out the guy just prolonged the pain; my friend had nightmares, she couldn't eat properly, and she was screwing up so badly at work that she was worried she would lose her job.

I have no idea what planet this guy is from, or what jail he broke out of. All I know is he had no shame or honor, and he was capable of doing anything as long as it suited his selfish desires.

I wish I could tell you this guy was like Mr. Big from *Sex and the City* and changed his mind. I wish I could tell you my friend was Carrie Bradshaw and got her happy ending. But in the real world there are sad endings, and in the real world there are selfish pricks that women need to dump.

These days when I see female friends dating selfish jerks, all I can do is give them advice and tell them they're dating an asshole. But it's futile to tell a girl she should really break up with the guy she's dating. At the end of the day, the only person who can make that decision is the girl; she has to be the one to decide that the pain is not worth it, and she needs to move on.

Good Riddance

Let's assume you've been dating an asshole, and you finally decided to kick him to the curb and out of your life. Want to know the quickest way to stop the pain and forget the guy? Do the following, and it'll speed things up.

1) **Let Go**. You've realized the guy is a jerk and has serious character flaws, so don't look back. Do not blame yourself for what happened. Do not wonder if you could have done anything differently that would have made the relationship work. The guy was a scorpion, so let go and for the love of God, do not hope he will change and come back to you!

2) **Throw Away Everything**. If he's got clothes in your place any lingering scents will keep you thinking about him. Throw away all photos and things you bought together; all they'll do is invoke memories of the guy. Any expensive gifts should be returned to the guy via a friend, or give it to charity or someone poor. It's only when you remove all remnants of the guy from your life that you can move on.

3) **No Contact**. Until you are completely over the guy, avoid all contact. If the guy's an asshole, he'll try to contact you, and probably run the crying game on you. He's either lonely and thinking of himself, or he's so dumb and selfish he doesn't realize he's making it harder for you to move on. If he calls, be polite and tell him the two of you need to stop talking so you can move on. If he still keeps calling, then tell him this: "If there was any justice in this world, you're going to end up shoveling shit in hell!" Hopefully he gets the point then.

4) **Focus on Yourself**. It's normal to feel sad or depressed after a break-up, but the worst thing you can do is sit at home all alone. Now is the time to go out and enjoy life. Go out with friends and have some fun, but don't get drunk! Go try things you've always wanted to do but didn't have time for before because you were too busy dating. Try windsurfing or hiking if you're sporty, and if you're not, then go join a club or learn to paint. Do something to preoccupy your mind so you think about the guy less.

5) **Participate in Sports**. When you exercise, your body will produce endorphins, which is a natural pain killer. It's why they say runners sometimes get a "runner's high," because the feeling after a workout is so good. Endorphins have been

known to help people with mild depression, so naturally if you're feeling bad, exercising can help take your mind off things and make you feel better.

Breaking up is never easy, even if it's with the biggest jerk. But there is one good thing about breaking up: now that you're single, it means you have the opportunity to meet someone new that does suit you and treat you right!

PART 2

How to Attract Decent Men

Chapter 13

What Everyone Wants

For the remainder of this book, I'll discuss how a woman goes about attracting a decent man, and I'm going to do it in the most honest, no-bullshit way possible. It might not be what you want to hear, but its stuff that actually works.

Women often get together and give each other advice on men based on what they think their friends want to hear, because it sounds so sweet and good. But it's not necessarily what actually works. To be honest, it's like the blind leading the blind, so I'm going to avoid doing the same thing.

If you want an attractive man, then the first thing you need to do is be honest about what you want. Off the top of their heads, a lot of women often say all they want is a nice guy, but that's not being completely honest. Women also want a man they can respect, a man who's interesting to be with, a man who makes them feel safe and secure, and a man who's not a financial burden.

A nice guy who's boring won't cut it, and a nice guy who grovels for your attention and you don't even respect him, just doesn't cut it. A girly-boy who makes you look like Xena the warrior princess and him, your little bitch, just doesn't cut it.

It's the pursuit of attractive male qualities such as an interesting personality, confidence, wit, and a good sense of humor that causes many women to end up with assholes. Bring the best of both groups together, however, and you've got a man who's attractive, and will treat you well. That's what I mean by a decent guy.

Okay, I know some of you are going to challenge me on this. I know there will be women out there questioning how an asshole could possibly know what decent men want, and it's a fair challenge.

Well, although I'm an asshole, I'm still a man. In fact if I was a woman, I would know exactly what it takes to both seduce a man and keep a man interested. Not that I would want to, the idea of my face on a woman's body makes me want to throw up in my mouth.

Besides, I have lots of friends that are decent men. My best friend is a great husband, is a good father to two kids, and has a decent job. He's smart, he's fun, he's interesting, and everyone around him likes him and respects him. He's the complete package.

Unless a woman's bullshitting, if she can get herself a decent man, she will go for it. There are two problems, though, when it comes to decent men.

1) As I mentioned in chapter one, there aren't enough decent men out there. So to get one of these guys, you need to beat all the other girls. The competition is invisible because you don't know who they are, but it's there never-the-less. If you don't want to compete, then it's easy. Just find a boring guy; they're everywhere. You don't even need to read the rest of this book! But if you want the best, then you need to accept that there are other girls trying to get the attention of the guy that you like.

2) It's a two-way street. Just because a guy's not an asshole, it doesn't mean he doesn't have his own requirements, it doesn't mean he's a frigging charity and will go for any girl.

The more attractive a man is, the higher his requirements will be.

I'm sorry if I have to stick to reality. I'd like to sell you idealistic bullshit, but then it would be . . . . well, bullshit, and then you'll fail in your endeavors. Before you can find love with a guy, you need to attract the guy. The truth and the reality is that all human beings are the same, and I mean men and women.

When we pick partners we aim to get the best we can get

What a person can get differs between individuals. If I was a boring guy and women have been ignoring me all my life, and I can't get dates, then I'll probably be very happy to go date the first girl who shows interest in me.

If I was a really attractive guy, however, and I've got girls constantly flirting with me, then it's only natural that I'm going to pick the best. If I could get a girl who's interesting, is pretty, and has a nice personality, why would I just go for a girl who's pretty but a bitch? Why would I settle for less?

That's reality, and when I tell girls this, some say, "That's so sad!" Hey, it's not sad; you've been doing the same thing all your life. The feelings you have when you start liking a guy is nature's way of telling you a man is worthy of your time. You've got your own standards, and I can't force you to date a guy for which you don't have feelings. So why would you expect a decent guy to go for the first girl who comes along?

I think some girls think it's sad because they think they're not good enough to get themselves a decent guy, which is not true. Every girl can get herself a decent man if she wanted to, but a girl still needs to compete, and she has to be proactive about it. Like everything else in life, there are no free lunches out there, so it pays to accentuate as many of the qualities that men like as possible.

How to Get a Man to Fall in Love

This brings me to a key point. A lot of girls ask me, "What is it that makes a guy fall in love with one girl and not another?" The answer is pretty simple, but hard to execute. It happens in three stages. First you need him to feel physically attracted to you. Then you need to make him feel you are special and unique and better than the other women around him. Last you need to make him feel that his life is better with you in it than without you. Basically you need to make the guy think he's got himself a good catch.

If you make him feel like he's got a good catch, then the guy will start to think about you all the time, he'll want to be with you, and he'll naturally fall in love. Each man might have slightly different preferences, but in the following chapters I will explain the type of characteristics the vast majority of men find attractive in women.

But this does not apply to assholes!

Don't come back to me later and complain you've done everything in the second half of this book, and a guy's still not in love with you, and then it turns out the guy's the biggest player in your city! I already mentioned before: assholes only truly love themselves.

So here's my disclaimer:

The stuff I'm going to teach you will only work if the man has a healthy attitude about relationships. If you turn a blind eye to all the warning signs that you got yourself a massive dickhead, I'm not responsible for you failing!

Chapter 14

How and Where to Hunt

For some women, getting attention from an attractive male, any sort of attention, is still better than being alone. Even if it's short term, a booty call, and the guy treats the girl like dirt, it's still better than being lonely. These women have it all wrong.

It's this type of thinking that keeps a woman wondering why men don't hang around afterwards. The problem women have is not that they can't attract men in the first place. The problem is getting *commitment* and *respect* from the men they attract.

If you always have men disappearing on you after short hook-ups and you are tired of it, then you need to add more focus on getting commitment and respect. I don't want to be dramatic, but you need to tell yourself you simply won't tolerate players anymore, that you will execute the need to pursue this clear-cut goal with ruthless dedication.

When interacting with men, no matter how attractive the man is, if you're not going to get commitment and respect from a man, he's a waste of your time. Tell him to get out of your life! It's as simple as that. If you want a decent guy, then you need to focus, and that's going to be how you roll from now on, okay?

As you read through the following chapters, it's important to note that you're not doing any of the following because you need to impress a man. Think of it from a position of power. The following provides information about what men are attracted to, and you are empowering yourself with this knowledge so you can get what you want. You can pick and choose to cater to your own needs. Don't feel like you need to change yourself for someone else, because you won't be able to. The only way you're going to be able to apply any of the following is if you did it for yourself.

Be Nice to All Men

A lot of women, especially the ones that get hit on a lot, tend to reject the men they're not interested in immediately, and they give too much credit to the men they *are* interested in. I've lost count of the number of times I've walked up to a girl, and even before I opened my mouth, the girl gives me a disapproving look that says, "What the hell do you want?" Okay, I guess I'll have to accept that I'm probably butt ugly, and besides, I'm not a good example considering I'm an asshole. But is that look really necessary?

I understand it can be hard to give time to every guy if you get hit on constantly. But instead of rejecting men straight away, flip it around and do the opposite. There's something I've noticed about women who attract decent men: they tend to be friendly to all the guys around them, maybe not to some creepy dude who'll stalk them later, but to men in general they're really nice. After all, what do they have to lose by being nice?

Not all guys make a good first impression, and not all decent men are good looking. But when you write guys off too soon, you'll never find out if they're decent or not. It's much better to waste some time finding out that a guy's not your type, rather than falling in love with some good-looking asshole and wasting a few years on him.

Give a guy a chance, and be nice to all men. If the guy is not worthy enough, you can always reject him later.

It also pays to get out as much as possible and make the effort to meet as many guys as possible. Prince charming isn't going to drop on your lap if you're holed up at home. You want to have access to as many guys as possible so you have more choices from which to pick from.

Where to Look

Through Friends

Many people don't utilize their friends enough to try and get a date. While you are wondering where all the decent guys are, your friends might know decent guys out there wondering where the decent women are. It is by far the safest and most likely way to meet an eligible bachelor. Your friends also act as a good pre-filter, and the guy will know there is an element of accountability if he is out of line.

My best friend's wife takes pride in matching up people who could potentially fit well together, and I have to give it to her: thanks to her efforts three couples are now married, and a whole bunch more are dating.

A good friend like my friend's wife could be all you need. It could be a girl, or it could be a really close guy friend that'll watch out for your best interests. They'll help you find people and filter out most of the pricks.

Take care though, not all guys make good referrals. In fact a lot of guys make really bad referrals. I know guys who introduce the biggest assholes to their female friends. It's not because they want their female friends to get hurt; it's just that the guy making the introduction happens to be a dog himself, so he thinks it's okay for his guy friend to also be a dog.

Internet dating

Internet dating has become so big now that I had to list this as one of the main ways you can meet guys. The great thing about Internet dating sites is that you have access to a huge number of prospective males. The bad thing is that most people on online dating sites are shopping around, lots of people do a shotgun approach by mass messaging, and they might already be seeing other people. Still, if you have access to ten thousand men, even if 99 percent of them are assholes, that still leaves you a hundred decent men to work with. That's a lot!

Just be aware that you get all sorts of messed-up guys on these sites, from players to guys who are already married. In fact, as research for this book, I paid some ex-convicts to create some profiles and pretend they've got decent jobs, and they're now dating women out there! Are you one of them?

Nah, just messing with you, but you get the point. So be cautious when using this method.

There are a few rules when it comes to Internet dating.

Pictures. When posting up a picture of yourself it should be a good picture, taken from a nice angle and you should wear some attractive clothes. You should have a head and a body shot. But they have to be an accurate representation of you. It's amazing but a lot of people put up pictures of themselves from ten years earlier, studio shots that make them look totally different, or even pictures that have been air-brushed. A lot of people do this because they want to show themselves in a better light. But don't kid yourself.

If the picture doesn't look like you then when you show up, the guy's just going to think "what the fuck?", and he'll be pissed off he's been duped. A lot of men do the same thing by putting up fake pictures, and it's a big waste of everyone's time.

Profile Information. Your profile information should be similar to the way you would write out a resume to get a job. It should be to the point, rather than covering every little detail in your life. At the end of the day, the person who's surfing your profile doesn't have time to read dozens of life stories.

All information should be accurate but sound positive. Don't write negatives about yourself just to sound honest. Being honest doesn't mean you have to list that you like shopping at the mall on Sundays! You have to get the guy to like you and have him under your thumb and totally whipped before dragging him along to go shopping with you. Also, do not get sexual in your profile; don't write about sexual preferences, or how you like sex. Some women do this because they think they'll get more attention, but all they get are guys who want to have a one-night stand.

Never Initiate Contact. A girl should never message a guy even if she's interested. A guy needs to think you're special, and if he does he'll naturally contact you. If you message a guy first, you might get a date, but you'll risk a high failure rate later.

Protect Yourself. Just because it's a dating site doesn't mean men are looking to date. There are tons of men on dating sites just looking to hook up. Also, you know nothing about the man; everything in his profile could be a lie, so the time taken to get to know any guy you meet on a site should be extensive. There have been horror stories of women who have met men on these sites, and subsequently been robbed or raped after taking these men home.

Clubs and bars

Clubs and bars are melting pots of normal people just having fun, players, assholes, and the scumbags of the universe. They are the training grounds of players, so you'll probably wonder why I included them here. The reason is because several of my friends have met boyfriends through clubs, and there are people I know that have met their spouses in a club or bar. But I would only recommend clubs and bars to extremely street smart women. By "street smart" I mean a woman who can accurately assess the games men play.

Clubs are a high traffic, but high-risk environment because there are a lot of men having fun but a large percentage of the men are just looking to play. The golden rule to remember about bars and clubs is that, *every guy is a player until proven otherwise*. The key is to be in control of the situation if you meet a guy from a club, which can be hard if you're drunk. If you're just looking for a casual hook up that's your call, but exercise caution if you're going to go on a date. Have fun with a guy if he asks you out on a date, but you should reference everything I mentioned in the first half of this book to spot any early red flag behaviors.

Dating Agencies and Singles Events

A dating agency can help you speed up your search by locating someone of a similar social economic background or with similar interests. Also, because they require men to pay, and the meeting atmosphere is relatively serious, there are fewer players in such an environment. A less serious option is speed dating. But again, don't assume every guy you meet that makes a good first impression is a decent guy. The guy might not be playing but could still be an arrogant narcissist.

An Interest Group, Club or Church

Any sports club, dance class, coed sports team, or interest groups that bring both sexes together will be full of opportunities. It allows you to spend significant amounts of time with men who have a common interest, giving you time to get to know each other. They're fun and also allow you to meet more people, expand your social circle and give you more to talk about on a date.

By the way, don't go to church to look for men; go to church for God. I'm just saying if you already go to church, it seems like common sense to me that there'll be decent men there. It's strange though, whenever I tell girls to find men in churches I usually get blank stares. I've yet to figure out why; it's not like I suggested going for the pastor!

On Holiday, at Weddings, and Parks Where Men Walk Dogs

Yup, I'm referring to an earlier chapter, and just because I used a cheap trick it doesn't mean you write off the chance to meet men at those places. A lot of relationships have started from a casual conversation that started on a plane or in a park. Whenever a random guy initiates a conversation with you, don't write him off straight away; you've got nothing to lose and he could turn out to be interesting.

You should be flattered because the only reason he's approached you is because he thinks you're cute and attractive. It's a nice boost to anyone's self-esteem to know he or she is being pursued. Of course, don't get carried away either, especially if there's chemistry. Don't start over-romanticizing like you're the star in a chick flick.

Don't Try So Hard

Have you and your friends ever noticed that when you're not looking for a guy at all, a guy you click with will suddenly come along and find you? The reason this happens is because when you're not looking, you're more likely to just be out there having fun, enjoying yourself, and smiling. You will look more natural and happy. Get yourself out there so that you get a chance to interact with more guys, but make sure to have fun, that's when you look the most attractive.

Chapter 15

Confidence and Happiness

I went clubbing with my friend Carol and a group of her friends some time ago, and within the group there were two girls who were both pretty, so I sat there checking them out the whole night. Hey, that's normal for me.

But I wasn't just checking them out just because they were pretty. Usually when I go clubbing, in addition to having fun, I like observing the interactions between people. I don't know why I started doing this; I guess I've just found it fun to observe people when they're intoxicated and are more primal than in other social settings.

I was checking the girls out because I wanted to see the effect these two girls had on the men around them. After some time had passed, I noticed that while one girl had guys hitting on her the whole night, men stayed clear of the other girl.

The reason this happened was because the first girl was like a breath of fresh air. From a distance an observer could see the first girl smiling, laughing and having fun. The second girl didn't look happy; she looked serious or even moody, and thus a lot less approachable.

After talking to the second girl, I realized that in addition to being stressed out from work, she was pretty bitter about men. She'd had some bad relationships in the past and was resentful of men in general. I can understand if she was cautious, and the men who treated her badly were in the wrong, but her thinking didn't help her one bit; her negativity exuded from her in such a way that every guy avoided her.

She was a good example of a woman's mood affecting her attractiveness, and you'll be surprised how much a woman's internal state, how she thinks and feels affects her chances of finding a decent man. Below are some of the most significant things a woman can improve on to make herself more attractive to men.

Being Happy

Human beings, both men and women, are naturally drawn to those that are happy and fun to be with. Everyone wants to be happy, and being with happy and fun people is the easiest way to accomplish this. It's no surprise that men prefer women that come off as happy. Who wants to date a person that's miserable?

Now, if you're unhappy I don't presume to know why, and I don't want to belittle your situation or what you're going through. I do know, however, that a person can consciously decide to be happier. If I had a set back at work, I could sit at home and feel miserable, or I could go out with friends and have some fun. I could go watch a comedy and allow myself to smile and laugh. I could decide to be optimistic and not think of the negatives all the time.

Some people are naturally happy people and some are not, but to an extent we all have the ability to become happier people, and in turn become more attractive people. If you have things from the past that haunt you, put it all away and tell yourself you're going to have a new start!

Know That You're Hot Stuff

But you're not hot stuff, you say? Well, you've failed already if you think that way. Confident men attract more women, and women who know they're hot stuff naturally attract more men. Basically, you're more desirable if you think you're desirable.

Human beings are funny creatures. When we see someone of the opposite sex that's hard to get (hence where the term playing hard to get came from) we subconsciously attribute high value to that individual. People who are confident about their attractiveness to the other sex do two things.

1) When they interact with the opposite sex, even if they're attracted, they don't act desperate, so it becomes challenging to chase after such individuals. They might flirt but know that if the other person's not attracted, then they can back off and go look elsewhere, nothing lost and no harm done. In other words rejection doesn't hurt the pride of a confident person.

   The opposite of a confident person is a person who comes off as totally enamored and comes on way too strong, way too early. When people are lacking in confidence, every time they approach the opposite sex and feel attracted, they are prone to doing too much to impress, and to hopefully get the other person to like them. This only has the opposite effect, scaring off the target because it indicates the person is desperate and is therefore low in value.

   Despite what you hear in romance stories, professing your love verbally or through actions too early doesn't work. It backfires really badly.

2) These people know they have options. Therefore they're willing to take their time, to check a person out carefully before making a move, rather than dive headfirst into a relationship with anyone they feel attraction for. Girls who date assholes again and again lack this type of self-control

and decide to go for a guy whenever there seems to be some chemistry.

I don't mean to say that a girl should start acting like she's God's gift to mankind. What a girl should do is believe or know that she's attractive to a man that's she's with. There's no need to start chasing the guy, or to show that you're under his control in any way.

Overcome Loneliness

People who feel lonely or who fear being alone in the future can sometimes come off as being less attractive. The reason is they tend to act over-eager when they're interacting with someone they like. These people want to get rid of the lonely feeling so much, and find a partner so badly that it lowers their value significantly. They also tend to make their own situation worse, because they're so eager to get rid of the lonely feeling they are willing to put up with a man or woman who is behaving badly.

You ladies should know that better than anyone, because when an over-eager guy approaches you, you can literally sense the desperation. But confidence is so sexy, right?

I know what it feels like to be lonely. As I'm writing this, I haven't been in a relationship with a woman for almost a year. I've been working and writing and just haven't bothered to go out and meet girls. In fact I told a couple of female friends I hadn't had sex in seven months (by choice) and they looked shocked "That's not you! What's wrong with you? Are you okay? Do you need to see a doctor?"

To understand their concern, you have to realize me not chasing girls and having sex is like a fat kid standing in a candy store and he's not buying any candy. But it's part of my fifty-six step AA rehabilitation program (Assholes Anonymous) so I have to follow it.

It sucks to be lonely, and up to a point, we all wish we could be with someone who connects with us and truly understands us. But being lonely is the same as being unhappy. You could let it overwhelm you, or you can decide to beat it. So if you're lonely, here are some things you can do to stop it.

1) Take some time off from dating men. There's a lot more to life than just finding a man. Spend a few weeks doing all the stuff that you love and makes you happy. Go on vacation with friends, pamper yourself, or pick up a new and interesting hobby. Spend time with your family, especially if you don't see them often. Once you feel as though it's possible to live a perfectly happy life without a guy, then ironically you'll be in much better shape to go find one. You'll be much more attractive to a man once you're back on the dating scene.

2) Stop thinking you need a perfect man to complete you, to make you happy, or to fill some sort of hole in your soul. The Greeks invented the idea of the soul mate. They said humans used to have four arms, four legs, and a single head with two faces. Fearing human's power, Zeus the King of the gods, split us all in half, condemning us to spend the rest of our lives searching for our other half just to complete ourselves.

What a load of crap! It's ideas like these that causes people to get desperate and needy, which ultimately makes them unhappy. You don't need a guy to complete you; you're complete already. You are your soul mate!

I once read a girl's status on Facebook that read, "Sigh, another Valentine's Day without a boyfriend" So this girl basically feels miserable every year leading up to and after Valentine's Day, just because society creates this pressure to find love. Don't be like that. Learn to love yourself and be happy by yourself first.

Healthy relationships involve two complete individuals that come together to build a future together. It doesn't involve two incomplete individuals trying to fill each other's gaps.

3) Get a pet, especially a furry one. A dog or a cat might not be a complete substitute for a man, but it's good to have a cute animal around the house to make the place feel less lonely.

4) If all of the above fails, do the following: GET A RABBIT!

Rabbit Vibrators are amongst the world's best selling vibrators with millions sold around the world annually. The vibrator has a rabbit shaped stimulator (hence the name of the vibrator) that is held near the clitoris. This can be done whilst the body is taken into the vagina, offering deep (oh yeah baby, DEEP!), penetration. These toys usually offer multiple shaft rotation speeds and different patterns of clitoral stimulation, allowing for an out of this world experience.

Quite simply put, *The Rabbit* is a marvel of human engineering. All the hundreds of thousands of years of human advancement had the sole purpose of bringing us to this pinnacle of human development . . . . you no longer need a man to plug that hole . . . . in your soul. Hey if it's good enough to be featured on *Sex and the City* then it's good enough for you!

A word of warning: Rabbit vibrators perform better than most men, so don't use it too much, or start talking to it. It's really unhealthy if you start talking to it. If you ever find yourself saying, "I love you!" to it, then put it away. Use it only enough so you can think more clearly before going out to find a man.

Chapter 16

Early Impressions

The key to making great first and early impressions with a guy is to know what works and what doesn't. But the problem is what works might not come naturally. A lot of people wrongly assume they should do exactly what they feel like early on, because the other person should like them for who they are; they feel if they don't do exactly what comes naturally, then they're playing games. That's not true.

I'll give you an example. I was reading a relationship forum, and there was this one guy who was bitching about how life sucked. He went on a date with a girl, and afterwards he called her and showered her with attention. He called her so much in fact, she got bored and stopped talking to him.

The guy had no idea how the girl felt about him. Maybe later if they started having a relationship then he could have called whenever he wanted, but at the beginning no matter how badly he wanted to inundate her with calls, he should have known that calling a girl whenever he thought about her would come off as desperate and annoying. If he used a different approach the next time and exercised self-control, that's not game playing, that's just being smart and not scaring the girl off.

The same applies for you. Guys you meet don't know anything about you. You could be the most wonderful person in the world, but if you give a bad early impression, then you'll scare off the guy and he'll never find out. Sometimes I hear women complain about their bad luck with men. There's no such thing as bad luck, just bad strategies. Using the most effective strategies is not manipulation. Manipulation is when you're lying and leading someone on even if you're not interested. Effective strategies simply involve putting the best foot forward and figuring out how to effectively leverage your most attractive side so you get a guy attracted. You get more dates with the guy, and then he becomes hooked.

Smiling and Flirting

A lot of women use the wrong balance when it comes to flirting with men. They're either too forward, which makes them lose value in the guy's mind, or they're too shy and don't get a guy's attention. Obtaining the right balance is the key to success.

First of all, there's never a need to chase a guy. I don't care if you think he's the hottest stud you've ever seen in your life, and you want to get it on with him like there's no tomorrow. If you chase a guy, you eliminate yourself immediately. You may have heard this before, but men are hunters. The most you should do is flirt, if we like a woman we'll naturally chase.

Whenever a woman proactively chases a guy instead of him chasing her, even if she gets him, she runs the risk that he doesn't think of her as special. She's lowered her value in his subconscious mind, and that might lead to major problems later on because he'll lose interest weeks or months later. Men are easy to get, and the one thing worse than not getting him in the first place is getting him, but he doesn't commit later on because he doesn't treasure you.

It doesn't matter if you think this is a new millennium and women should be able to do whatever they want. You can do what you like, but that doesn't mean it'll work. You can't change animal nature. Chasing a guy is a low-success strategy, so let's just stick to what works. This is where effective flirting comes in.

Most guys experience fear when approaching women to which they're attracted. They're scared of rejection. In fact sometimes this fear is so strong that a guy who's interested might not approach a woman at all.

But it's really easy to lower this fear in a guy and get him to approach you. All you have to do is make eye contact with a guy, and maintain it for two to three seconds and give him a sweet smile. It's really that simple, and if he still doesn't approach, then he's either chickenshit, or stupid.

Either way you've lost nothing, and it's his loss. Don't take it badly and move on. Have the guts to smile at a guy in the first place, and if he approaches, feel free to smile a lot when talking to him. Just make sure you don't lick your lips when smiling at the guy, you're going to get a completely different and unintended effect!

Flirtatious Touching

If a guy approaches and the two of you have some chemistry, or if you had a good time on a date, you can use another effective strategy. Some girls actually do this without realizing it. If you playfully hit a guy or the arm, or make a light touch to his arm or chest, that'll increase the attraction level even more. A woman touching a man is a natural turn-on. Or you can simply just allow the distance between the two of you to decrease so that you're in each other's personal space. Men are easy to turn on; it doesn't take a lot of verbal flirtation to get a guy interested. Body language does the trick most of the time.

You've got to be observant though. If you're attracted to him, but he's not attracted to you, doing this backfires. Also, when I say touch, I mean the lightest of touches. If you go stroking the guy's chest that might turn him on, but it'll lower your value in his mind. You don't want him to think you're easy; you want him to think you're special.

Physical Attraction

I know it gets tiresome to some women. You girls buy high heels to make yourselves taller and make your legs look slimmer. You have put on make up to accentuate your features and cover some things up. Some of you buy push up bras to make your breasts look bigger. You buy nice dresses that hug your hips and your ass so when you walk past, men go "damn!"

You're conditioned to buy all these products by society, and half the stuff you do in the morning everyday is about making yourself look more beautiful. Then you go on a date, and you feel like some asshole is only interested in your breasts instead of you the whole night.

So it's no surprise to me that a lot of women ask the following questions: "Are men really that shallow? How important are looks? If you want to get a decent man, how hot do you have to look?"

I'm not going to lie, men are visual creatures, it's the way nature made us. Looks matter, and any woman who tells herself looks shouldn't matter at all is just kidding herself. It's generally true, that the better looking a woman is, the better her chances are of being approached by men.

But then again it's also true that you don't need to be hottest girl in town. If it was only about looks, then men would only settle down in relationships with the hottest women they've ever seen, and I know plenty of men who didn't marry the hottest woman they ever dated. Looks act as the hook to get the initial interest, and then decent men look a lot more at a woman's personality.

But to get the initial attraction, you still need to be relatively attractive. "Relatively attractive" is a subjective term, and I use it because how good looking you need to be varies depending on your competition. If you're in a really competitive city like New York, L.A, or Miami then looks matter more, simply because there are a lot of good-looking women around. If you're in a smaller town, the competition tends to be less.

What is universally true is that every woman should put effort into looking her best. Every woman can be relatively attractive if she wants to and makes the effort. Every woman should know how to take care of her skin properly, apply make-up properly, and get a nice hair cut that suits her. Every woman should also exercise enough to keep her body looking physically attractive.

A woman should learn to dress to kill on a night out, that means wearing heels and clothes that hugs her curves and shows off the shape of her breasts, hips, and bum, while not revealing too much skin. Leaving just enough for imagination is the biggest turn on for men. There are plenty of women's magazines that teach women how to do all this, so there should be no excuses not to make the effort.

I'm sorry if you don't agree with doing all this just to get a man interested. It's cool if you do none of it, but then again you shouldn't complain if you don't put in the effort and fewer men approach you. You can't change men, but you can change yourself to attract more men.

I know looks is a sensitive topic for a lot of women, but that's because ladies look at women's magazines, and in these magazines there are women who look perfect, and after a while all those images can start to hurt one's self-esteem. But, ladies, did you know there are three billion women in this world who don't look like supermodels, and only about twenty that actually do without editing the photos? The vast majority of men and women are in the same boat.

If it makes you feel better, even I have to bust my ass just to maintain myself. When I first started writing this book, I drank so much beer, ate so much junk food, and did so little exercise that I developed a serious beer belly. It got so bad that I went hiking once and my female friends made fun of me afterwards because when I was coming down the mountain they could see my belly bounce up and down.

Not a pleasant image, I know, and it wasn't cool either when I went out at night. Girls would rub my belly and laugh because I looked like I was six months pregnant. So I stopped making excuses for not exercising and got back in shape. We can all do it. It's not easy, sometimes I lose self-control and eat half a cow for dinner, but the important thing is I make an effort on most days.

The Curse of the Beautiful Woman

Just a word of advice, and I'm saying this so I don't sound completely shallow. Don't starve yourself just to look better. I'd hate to have some girl read this and feel pressured to lose weight only to become anorexic.

Besides, hot doesn't guarantee success. Some of the most miserable women I know are actually really hot. Some of the hottest women I know and I'm talking about models, have the lowest success rate in keeping men interested. They get hit on a lot but fail in relationships over and over again, and I'll tell you why.

They fail because they rely on looks too much. They're hot so they get hit on by some of the most charismatic and charming men out there, and they tend to lose interest in less outgoing men. But the problem is they're so used to men drooling all the time that they neglect to work on things that men are into, like conversations that go beyond "whatever" and "You know what I mean?"

Men will feel compelled to approach attractive women. Use your looks to attract a guy, but then it's your personality and your cunning ability to read what he wants that keeps the man next to you.

Playing Hard to Get

Human psychology 101: if something is harder to get, we treasure it more. Think of diamonds; they might be pretty, but they're not that much prettier than other shiny stones. But they call diamonds a girl's best friend. Why? They are expensive, and hard to get, that's why. If diamonds looked exactly the same but were sold for a dime a dozen on the street corner, they would no longer have the same desired effect.

Playing hard to get might seem like game playing and manipulation, but you're actually trying to replicate how a confident individual acts. As I mentioned before, confident individuals know they have options and don't act over enamored when they like someone. They don't kiss up to the people they like. They don't act as though they need that person because it gets rid of their loneliness. That in turn makes them seem higher in value to a prospective mate. If you really believe you're hot stuff, you wouldn't even need to play hard to get, you *will* be hard to get.

Here's the secret to playing hard to get. *In order to increase your chances of getting a man to feel you're special you have to be confident enough in yourself to risk losing the guy.*

There are a few things you can do to achieve this goal.

1) When a guy is still chasing you, and he calls, e-mails, or texts, do not respond immediately. Wait at least a couple of hours before responding, or if it's late at night respond the next day. That makes him anticipate your response so he thinks about you; it also shows that you're busy with work or other stuff, and he's not important enough to get you at his beck and call. Continue to live your own life!

   The other night my friend Emma received a call from the guy she liked while having dinner with me and another girl. She picked up immediately and proceeded to have a fifteen-minute conversation with the guy; she even walked off at one point. Not that I took offense, because I was busy stuffing my face with her share of the food. But it was her loss for being so available to the guy; it would bite her in the ass if the guy lost interest later on because the chase was too easy.

2) At the beginning do not have long conversations on the phone, and don't text or e-mail the guy frequently. Do not see the guy all the time even if he wants to see you. Limit the number of times you see the guy to twice a week at the beginning. I know this will be tough, because if you like him you'll naturally want to see him or talk to him, but you want him to think about you all the time. Too much contact reduces this feeling, and at the beginning you don't want familiarity to happen too quickly.

3) Do not have sex with the guy too soon. Yeah I know, blah, blah, don't have sex too soon. Sue me ok? It works. I'm sorry if you just want to have a little fun, but you don't want to come off as easy.

   If you're horny, then bring out the Rabbit, or go to a bar or a club. All you need to do is pass a note around that you'll have "no strings attached" sex with the first man who will leave the club with you, and a line will form.

   Yeah, it's easy for a woman to get sex, in fact dick is free and comes with free drinks. But getting a man to feel like he'll give up the world just to be with you is not, so do not have sex with a guy till you're sure he really likes you.

4) When interacting with the guy, don't start going out of your way to please him. Let him know you may have some interest in him, but don't give him the feeling you're so interested in him you'll do anything to impress him. In fact, act indifferent until you see that he's really interested in you first.

5) If you're the type that often becomes infatuated with a guy once you start liking him, then you need to back off a little. Until you're in an exclusive relationship with the guy, if there are other men after you, feel free to go on dates with them. This is not something you do to make the guys jealous. This is something you do for yourself so that you are reminded that you're desired by other men, and it also allows you to think more clearly so if the guy you like is in fact an asshole, you haven't put him on a pedestal and are more likely to spot red flag behaviors.

Trust me, playing hard to get works, and if you still don't believe me, ask yourself this. Do you really want to date someone who was easy to get? Would you really want to say the following to your friends? "Yeah my man is a scrub. I beat him around the head and spat in his face multiple times. In fact I set his car on fire, and he's still kissing my ass!"

I really doubt you would want to date such a person. But although playing hard to get works, there needs to be a skillful balance. Men do not like bitches. Playing hard to get doesn't mean disrespect or treating a man with sheer malice. Not returning texts for a few hours is okay, but not returning texts for a week is a mistake.

Generally the more confident a man is, the better playing hard to get works. An alpha male will treat playing hard to get as a challenge and respond really well, whereas playing hard to get on a shy guy usually backfires and he'll think you're not interested.

It takes skill to judge the interest level of the guy. Like fishing, you need to hook a guy and then keep just enough tension in the string. You don't want to let the string slacken, and you don't want to pull too hard and let the string break.

I should also state this stuff is just for the beginning to generate attraction. Later when you're in a loving relationship, don't use these techniques because they can cause more harm than good.

Chapter 17

The Art of Conversation

If you asked me who is the most interesting person I've ever met, I would have to say it's my friend Mike. He's a very outgoing, and funny guy, and it's always fun to hang out with him. Mike also happens to be below average height, and if you ask Mike how he developed his confidence and sense of humor, he'll tell you it's because he's not tall.

He had to develop coping mechanisms to compete with bigger guys. He learned to make interesting conversation and to be funny in order to meet women, and he uses humor to defuse the situation or put down bigger guys who challenge him. Mike basically had to learn to better himself in order to compete because the world drove him to.

If you asked me who was the most boring person I've ever met, I would have to say it was this really hot girl I went out for dinner with a few years back. In fact she was so boring I can't even remember her name. She had nothing to say, no opinions about anything, and half the time I felt like I was talking to myself. I was really physically attracted to her, but I was bored shitless.

Now I'm not insinuating that beautiful women are boring to talk to. I'm not about to piss off every beautiful woman in the world. I'm an asshole but I'm not stupid. My point is that making interesting conversation and being funny can actually be learned if a person puts his or her mind to it, and for any woman out there who wants a decent guy, being interesting is crucial. If a woman is hot but boring, it doesn't matter how many dates she gets; guys will eventually lose interest over time.

The importance of conversation varies depending on how outgoing the guy is. If a guy is relatively quiet and shy, and you don't talk much then he probably won't care as much. But if you go on a date with a guy that's got a lot to talk about then you have to make it interesting for him as well.

Have Opinions and Don't be Shy

Some girls are very interesting people once a guy gets to know them, but on a date they freeze up because they get nervous. There's nothing to get nervous about. Remember at the beginning that you're the one in the selector role, not him. Just imagine you're going to a job interview, except you're the interviewer, and he's your bitch for the night because he needs to impress you.

Every time I get interviewed, I'm always a little nervous, and that's normal. But every time I've interviewed someone for work, I've always gone in with a sly grin on my face, because I know the other person's there to impress me.

Once on the date it's also important to have opinions. Although you don't want to be over-opinionated and come across as annoying, you still need to be engaging. If a guy asks you what type of food you like to eat, don't just say, "I'm good with whatever you're having," or "I don't really mind." Yes, no, or "I don't know" just doesn't cut it. Have a view on things to make things interesting for the guy.

Don't Talk Excessively About Yourself

The opposite of a girl who has few opinions is a girl who keeps on rambling about herself and every aspect of her life, who doesn't even give the guy a chance to talk. A conversation has to go both ways in order to be interactive and interesting.

I know plenty of guys who do this as well. They just keep talking and talking. Typically a guy starts talking about something he likes, but then it starts getting really long-winded, and everyone is sitting there either with their mouths hanging open in awe at how much crap can come out of his mouth or has fallen asleep, but because he's so self-centered he hasn't even noticed. Avoid doing this on a date.

Don't Sound Bored

If the guy is boring then it's going to be hard to not sound bored. But it's also your responsibility to keep things interesting. If you go to a date with low energy levels and act bored from the very start, then that feeling could just spread between the two of you. One of the ways to avoid doing this is to sound interested, maintain a high energy level, and avoid talking in a monotone voice.

Human beings convey more in their voice tonality than in what is actually being said. For example, if you see someone, you can say, "Hey, how's it going?" in a dull voice, or "Hey! How's it going?" in an excited, happy tone. The difference is huge.

If you don't believe me, go get a tape recorder and tape a conversation or two. Interesting people vary their tone, pitch, and volume throughout a conversation. If you show energy in your conversation, the other person will have more energy. If you've got a boring tone, then the other person will get bored. Having said that, don't start talking like you're a kid with attention deficit disorder and on a sugar high. Those women are scary . . . .

Expand Your General Knowledge

You don't need to be super intelligent to get a smart and interesting guy, but it pays to have knowledge on a broad range of subjects, to be aware of current affairs; it gives you the option to have more topics to talk about on a date.

But stay away from religions and politics or any subject that could turn into a debate, or even worse, a heated argument. From personal experience, religion and politics on a date is recipe for disaster, simply because different people have different views and beliefs when it comes to religion and politics. The last thing you want is to get each other kicked out of the restaurant because you started killing each other.

Making Conversations Interesting

On a lot of dates, things start off well, and then after going through all the normal topics people talk about, there's a risk for a lull in the conversation. If that happens don't count on the guy to lead the conversation. If you can both have a lot to talk about, the conversation flows like magic. The art of conversation comes from the ability to bring up creative topics and to bridge them.

- **Interest and Hobbies**. "So what sports do you like?" "Oh, you like horror movies? What's your favorite?"
- **People of Significance**. "Since you don't like your boss, if you could play a practical joke on him, what would it be?"
- **Dreams and Goals**: "What's your dream job?" "If you could take us anywhere in the world right now, where would it be?"
- **Past Experiences**. "What's your fondest memory from your childhood?" "What's the scariest thing that's ever happened to you?"

There are a lot of topics you can't bring up randomly. There needs to be a bridge to get to them, or the guy will go "Huh?" For example, you can't go from talking about the food to horror movies. But you can ask him if he's watched any movies lately, and then move on to that question. It's like doing word association games: you find a link from one topic to another and then move on to the next; all there has to be is one link.

Be Funny or Tease the Guy

Teasing a guy has multiple functions. If a guy is really confident or even cocky, teasing him is like a fun and harmless slap that brings him down a couple of levels. Teasing the guy can make the date less serious and more lighthearted. If the joke is witty and funny, it makes you look intelligent and fun to be with. Teasing can also be used to test how a guy responds to pressure: Will the guy flip out? Will he get butt-hurt? Or is he also witty and able to make a comeback?

Give you an example. Some time ago I was out on a date with a girl who was a lot younger. In fact she was eight years younger than me. We started talking about sports and athletes, and she told me she once had a conversation with a former pro athlete, and the guy was complaining about how after thirty a man slowly loses his ability to maintain the same strength and fitness level.

She was telling me how the guy mentioned he couldn't sprint as fast and was finding it harder to take hard blows from contact sports. Then after about two minutes of explaining what the guy had told her, she casually mentioned, "Actually I think the guy was probably the same age as you . . . ."

It cracked me up. She knew I was a lot older than her, and she spent two minutes talking about a subject just to lead to a punch line, which was meant to tease me about my age.

Obviously, teasing a guy can backfire if the guy has no sense of humor or can't lighten up. But if that's the case, then maybe you wouldn't want him in the first place. Don't go overboard on the teasing, which might actually offend the guy, but a modest amount of joking, teasing, and witty banter are things that can make a date a lot more fun and make the guy think you're better than other girls he's met.

Lighten up. A good sense of humor comes from practice and not worrying too much about what other people think. Men like funny women, too.

Chapter 18

Seducing with Sex

Warning: If you're pregnant, suffering from high blood pressure, on medication, or one of those ladies that faints whenever someone uses the word "sex", then the following chapter isn't for you. However, if you want to know exactly how to drive a man totally crazy for you by using sex, then read on.

About two thousand years ago a woman did an incredible thing. She seduced two of the most powerful men in Roman history, Julius Caesar and Mark Anthony. These men were so powerful they commanded tens of thousands of troops in battle, and could order the death of someone with a click of a finger. That woman was Cleopatra, the Egyptian queen.

According to historical sources, Cleopatra was not an incredibly beautiful woman, but she had a very seductive personality, and she knew how to use sex and sex appeal to her advantage. In fact women who knew how have used sex as a tool to seduce men throughout the ages, and you can use it, too.

I've mentioned several times in this book not to have sex with a man too early, for various reasons. When you do have sex with a guy, however, then you should go all out. Don't make any half measures, and don't get shy; you want to make sure it's the best he's ever had.

I know a lot of girls are shy when it comes to sex, or they don't want to think of it in such a primal way; they want to call it making love, which is cool. You can call it sex, making love, sleeping together, or making babies, it's all cool. The problem is the physical act itself is going to either be good or bad. There's "blow his mind" love making, good love making, bad love making, and "epic fail" love making, and the last thing you want is to have the guy walk away after making love thinking the experience really sucked.

Good sex is not going to be the only factor that will keep a man next to you, but it's still a big factor, and the best way to get a guy interested is to know what turns men on and what turns them off.

The Lady and the Slut (Hell Yeah Baby!)

This means being a lady in public. Any decent guy out there would want their female partner to be respectable in public. This is especially true if the guy takes his girlfriend to see his mum or to public functions and parties. No decent guy wants to be seen with a woman who acts brainless or slutty in public.

At home, however, the opposite is true. It doesn't mean you have to act like a slut per se, but the more adventurous you are and the more responsive you are to the guy, the better the sex will be. In other words, men love women who genuinely love sex.

Adventurous means willing to experiment with different positions, willing to have sex in pretty much every room in the house, and possibly dressing up for the guy.

Responsive simply means not being a dead fish. One of the biggest turn-ons for a guy is seeing a girl who's passionate in bed, making sounds and moving around.

Different girls make different sounds, some girls whimper, some girls scream, and some girls sound like they just stubbed their big toe. As long as you don't start barking like a dog, it's all cool. Be responsive; the biggest turn-off is having a woman who's all limp and shit, no guy likes to feel like he's crap in bed (even if he is).

The Lady and the Lady (Only if the guy sucks too)

It's nice to have a girl that's a lady in public, but if she's also shy in bed that's going to be a problem. It might not be a problem at the beginning because the guy's into a girl, but after a while it just gets plain boring making love to a mannequin.

Sex is meant to be one of the greatest pleasures in life, so enjoy it! Have some response and don't lie on your back like a dead fish. Your only excuse would be if the guy's so bad, you can't even bring yourself to fake an orgasm, in which case you probably need to dump the guy.

The Slut and the Slut (Don't expect commitment)

The "slut and the slut" are girls who might be great in bed but they act like sluts in public, and they often complain about men treating them like crap. Let me explain why this happens.

I went on a day trip once with a large group of people, on a boat out to sea, and on that day a couple of the girls started going wild and totally crazy after drinking. One girl started making out with multiple guys on the boat. The other girl was caught straddling one of the guys who already had a girlfriend. He was in the wrong for letting her do it, but she was in the wrong for acting like a slut.

I'm sure these two girls just wanted to get some attention, and they *did* get attention. But when guys see girls act or dress too overtly sexual, those girls get classified in a zone in the guy's brain called the "I will fuck this chick then run" zone, and no decent guy will consider dating one of these girls long term.

The funny thing is, if I walked up to either of these girls and told them they were acting like sluts, I bet they would have slapped me and told me they weren't sluts. They're probably right too, it's not like they started having sex with multiple guys on the boat.

Just because they're acting like sluts doesn't mean they are sluts. But I have to tell you this . . . .guys tend to have a problem differentiating.

It would be as if I were to dress up like one of the Village People and then go down to a gay club, walk around smiling at all the guys in the club. But when a guy comes to chat me up, I slap him and tell him, "Just because I'm acting gay, it doesn't mean I am gay!"

Don't get mad at us for not being able to differentiate, okay? Some girls think that because men like sex, flaunting their stuff gets men interested. What they don't get is that men from miles away will be flock to them for sex but those men won't be looking for a long lasting relationship. After several weeks or months the guy will lose interest and move on.

The Slut and the Lady (Blasphemy)

This is the worst combination possible. If you're going to act like a slut in public and a dead fish in bed, then forget ever having a man. Not only will the sex be bad, but this constitutes misleading advertising, and that makes you as bad as a player pretending he's a nice guy.

Sex and Communication

When it comes to sex, probably the single most important thing is communication. Everyone has slight variations on what they prefer, what turns them on and what turns them off. But if you ask around, you'll find a lot of people are not satisfied with their sex lives. A lot of people have preferences but never tell their partners what turns them on because they are too shy to speak up, and a lot of people are often uncomfortable during sex, or even in pain because what their partner is doing doesn't feel right.

A lot of people are scared to speak their mind because they fear if they tell the truth then they'll hurt the other person's feelings. Which I think is totally crazy. Think of it this way. If you go to a restaurant and the food isn't cooked right, what do you do? Complain. If the service is bad, then what do you do? Complain. Yet there are people out there who don't complain when they're being poked the wrong way, and hurting like a bitch. It's just ridiculous . . . .

If you use constructive criticism, utilizing phrases like "I love it when you do this" or "It's kind of uncomfortable when you do that," a loving partner will understand and be accommodating.

When you first start having sex, it's a good idea to give directions on what feels good and what doesn't. That way your partner knows from the beginning what turns you on and what turns you off. Simply let your partner explore your body and tell him what to do, higher, lower, harder, or softer. Whatever it may be, be frank about it. When he gets it wrong, shake your head; when he gets it right, nod and moan in pleasure, and he'll know what's working. Do the same but reverse roles when you start exploring his body.

Don't be shy. If a loving relationship is about honesty, then being honest with each other about what feels good in bed is nothing to be ashamed of.

Teasing Prior to Sex

If you really want to turn a guy on, then you shouldn't wait for the guy to initiate sex each time. Girls who know how to seduce properly also know how to tease a guy so that a huge amount of anticipation and tension is built up in the guy. This makes the actual sex feel a lot more intense for the guy.

Here are the top ten ways to drive a man insane.

1) Send him dirty texts during the day about what you're going to do to him later that night. You'll know you've succeeded when he tells you to stop it because he can't focus on work anymore.
2) If you're in the elevator and he's standing in front of you, rub his butt. If you're standing in front of him, grind your butt against him. No one will see if the elevator's crowded and you're subtle about it.
3) When you're having dinner in a restaurant, run your feet along his leg or if you're really brave, sit next to him instead of across from him and start stroking him under the table. You know it's working when he chokes or can't eat properly.
4) When you get home from work, put on one of the shirts he wears to work or t-shirts and walk around with nothing else on.
5) While wearing something like a short skirt, pretend to drop something and then bend over to pick it up so that he gets to see your legs and ass.
6) Blindfold the guy, play some music, put on something he likes (lingerie or dress up as a cop or a nurse), and then take the blind-fold off. Lap dance is optional.

7) Nibble on a guy's ear; some guys really like this.
8) Don't let the guy undress himself; do it for him and make sure to stroke his package before taking his pants off.
9) When entering the bedroom, lead a guy by his hand as though you're the one dragging him in there.
10) Once it looks like you're definitely about to have sex, tell him in a teasing way you've changed your mind and he needs to catch you if he wants some. Be careful not to get hurt or break stuff if you're running around the house or apartment!

I guess points two and three might get you in trouble, so don't blame me if some old lady catches you rubbing your butt against your man and gives you a disapproving stare. I know a lot of these moves will seem crazy, but that's the point! Crazy stuff gets the adrenaline pumping and heightens the sexual experience. It's the opposite of boring routines that cause sex to become dull over time.

How to Give a Good Blowjob

There are hundreds of books about sex that have been written over the years. If I was to write everything there is to write about sex then this book will be at least 800 pages long, so I've picked out just one key component of sex to talk about, the blowjob.

If you ask around, you'll soon notice one of the areas where men underperform the most when it comes to sex is a lot of men cum way too soon. They've finished and the girl isn't even close to orgasm. When it comes to women not turning a guy on, the two main areas of complaints, are being unresponsive in bed (which I discussed already) and not knowing how to give a proper blowjob.

Most women assume they know how to give a blowjob, but I'm sorry ladies, most of you don't know how to give a good one. You know why? Most people are too scared to discuss details when it comes to sex, because even though we all do it, and many of us talk about it, details are still taboo for most people. Well fuck taboo. I'll take the heat and teach you instead, because if you want to drive a guy insane, then you need to know how to do it properly. When a woman really knows how to give a good blowjob, a guy will never forget the experience; it's stuck in his mind till he either dies or goes senile, that's how much impact it can have on a man, and any man who's ever received a really good blowjob will testify to that.

So how does a girl give a good blowjob? I suggest you stop reading right now if sex makes you squeamish. If you can't be mature about it, then don't read ahead. If you can't handle the sex tips section of *Cosmopolitan*, then you definitely won't be able to handle what you're about to read next. I don't want you to wake up in the middle of the night covered in a cold sweat, screaming, "No more blowjobs!" Only read on if you really want to know how to give an amazing blowjob:

1) The word *blowjob* came from the English Victorian slang "Below-job," but there's no blowing involved. Blow into a guy's dick, and you might need to take him to a hospital. A good blowjob involves a small amount of suction. Suck too hard and you're the one to blame if the guy starts foaming at the mouth. Don't suck at all, and you're pretty much doing nothing, that is, you need to suck so you don't suck. Each man's preference is different, so ask the guy what level of suction feels best.

2) No teeth! We're talking about a man's most prized possession here. It is not lunch!

3) Use your hand to stroke the shaft with a small twisting motion while giving the blowjob is a good variation. If he's too small for you to stroke at the same time as when you're sucking, I'm sorry to hear this and can't help you there. Start praying it gets bigger!

4) Alternate between slower and faster speeds, and try circling the head of the penis with your tongue. (Shit, I hope my mother never gets this far into the book!)

5) The penis is not the only sensitive area in that region. It pays to lick the inside of the guy's legs and the guy's balls. You've got to be careful though, a guy's balls are *really* sensitive. Instead of getting rough with a guy's balls you might consider sticking a six-inch blade into his thigh because it would not be as painful.

6) If you want to drive a guy insane with sexual tension, then start off by licking his chest, torso, and then down around his inner legs and everything else apart from his penis. When you're doing this yell questions at him like, "Who's your mama?" Don't give him what he wants unless he's literally begging for it and shouts back, "You're my mama! Now please start! Please!!!"

7) Alternate between mouthing and licking the penis. That means licking from the base of the penis to the top, then putting it in your mouth again.

8) If you make and maintain eye contact with the guy while giving the blowjob, that's a major turn-on for a lot of guys. Once he's fixated on you like a deer caught in the headlights, change the tempo from slow and deep to rapid fire and watch him pass out with pleasure.

9) Do not pause every twenty seconds; that will cause the guy to lose sexual tension. If you need air, then switch to licking instead of sucking.

10) Be passionate about it! You're not being punished for sins you committed in your last life! You might consider it a duty but that's the wrong way to look at it. You're there to please the man you're in a relationship with. How would you like it if you had sex with a guy who had a grimace on his face? If you really can't be passionate about it then you might as well put a paper bag over his head and just imagine you're going down on Brad Pitt or some other stud.

Remember, sex is good. Love it and enjoy it, and if you want to get a guy to really desire you, don't get shy when it comes to sex. There's more to a relationship than sex, but sex is an integral part, and you can't afford to neglect it.

*Lots of women told me after reading this chapter that I should teach men how to go down on a woman properly as well. I appreciate the feedback, and will write a section about that in my next book!

Chapter 19

Why a Guy Loses Interest

There's always that guy who seemed interested in a girl, and then all of a sudden for no apparent reason, he stops calling. I don't mean he cuts the girl off, but all of a sudden he stops chasing. It happens quite frequently: a girl's out on a date with a decent guy, and he's not looking to play around. She likes him and thinks there's chemistry between the two of them, and at the end of the date he's still smiling and everything seems good. But then he never calls back.

Why does this happen?

Well what happened is the same thing as what happens when a girl no longer wants to see a guy again. The girl probably did or said something wrong on the date, and it made the guy lose interest. It sucks, I know, but the good thing is if you understand men well enough you can identify what went wrong and avoid doing it again.

There are a few things that tend to scare the crap out of men and turn us off, and usually it's linked to our fear of losing our freedom.

Fear of Losing Freedom

Let me tell you a story to explain why men often run away from women. It all started at the beginning of time with Adam and Eve.

On the sixth day, God created man, and man was free. He was free to roam around the Garden of Eden doing pretty much whatever he liked. He walked around butt naked all the time, ate from whatever tree he wanted, did as he pleased, and life was good.

Then one day God decided that it was not good for man to be alone anymore, so he made Adam a helper. From one of Adam's ribs God created Eve, and for a time things were really good. Not only was Adam walking around butt naked and free as a bird. He now had a naked chick walking around with him. No man could possibly ask for more!

But alas, good things never last, and Adam and Eve were tricked by the serpent and cast out of the garden for eating from the tree of knowledge of good and evil.

Then life got hard. Adam could no longer do as he pleased; he had to till the earth to farm for food, to provide for himself and his family. It wasn't an easy task, plus now Eve was smart, so he had to provide the best for her or she would get pissed off and bitch at him.

That was not the only downside to Eve gaining knowledge. Now that Eve was smart, Eve knew how to make Adam feel guilty. Adam could no longer do as he pleased, he could no longer walk around butt naked, and every time he did something bad, he was fearful of Eve. He was scared Eve would cry and make him feel that awful guilty feeling again.

Adam couldn't handle this loss of freedom, so he tried to leave Eve, but Eve started clinging onto him, so Adam relented and stayed with her. So from that day onward, every generation of man after Adam was born with a natural desire for women, but also the fear of losing his freedom to a woman. On that day, every man became fearful of needy, clingy, materialistic, and bossy women.

Okay, I was just kidding around with that story. But I wanted to illustrate some key points about male psychology with this story. Before us men meet a woman, we're pretty much free to do whatever we want, and although we all desire women, we don't want to spend the rest of our lives with anyone that makes us feel like we no longer have our freedom.

To make a guy truly fall in love, you have to make him feel life is happier and more fulfilling with you in it than when he was by himself. The last thing the guy wants is to feel bossed around, or emotionally blackmailed. He shouldn't think he needs to take care of a girl who's emotionally reliant on him, so here are a few behaviors that consistently turn men off.

Clinginess and Neediness

A while back my friend Keith went out for dinner with a girl he'd been on a few dates with, and things went great on the date. Afterward he hung out with the girl's friends, and they all went clubbing together. I actually joined them for part of the night, and everything was cool, the girl seemed nice when I met her.

At the end of the night it was getting late, and he had to meet me and a group of other people early the next morning to go hiking, so he gave the girl a kiss and a hug and said he had to go. That's when it started getting all weird. Maybe the girl was drunk, but she wanted to go to his place, and when he said no because he needed to get some sleep, she started insisting.

He kept saying no, and she kept insisting till they had an argument on the street, and then she started crying. He just wanted to go home and get some sleep, but instead he felt like a total scumbag and had to comfort her. In the end he couldn't take it anymore. He left her with her friends, jumped into a cab, and stopped seeing her after that.

Neediness is suffocating. A lot of women can't stand needy men, but it works both ways. When a woman acts needy, she comes off as desperate; and for a guy to truly feel attracted to a girl, he has to respect her. It's also scary for the guy because the guy starts feeling like she can't find her own happiness, and he's become responsible for it, and if he doesn't give her the attention she wants, then she's going to make him feel guilty.

Lesson to be learned: when a guy asks you out on a date, he's already interested. In fact when you accept a date, be nice, hang up the phone, and then pump your fists in the air in triumph and shout, "Yes! I've got that sucker by the balls!"
He's interested in you so, why sweat it?

In fact bookmark this page and in future before going out on a date flip to this page and repeat after me:

YES, I'VE GOT THAT SUCKER BY THE BALLS!
I'M NO 1!
I'M NO 1!
I'M NO 1!

Remember, you have to pump your fists up in the air when you say this . . . .

I completely understand: during or at the end of a date, a girl who's attracted might want reassurance that the guy feels the same way about her, but any sign of clinginess will simply drive the guy away. Remember, a girl who knows she's hot stuff will be confident in the belief that if she can't get this particular guy, there are others out there.

You can't pressure the guy into liking you no matter how much you like him; instead the opposite works best. Show that you're somewhat interested but don't really give a shit.

Being Put on the Spot

Some women, especially if they're meeting men via the Internet or through dating agencies, tend to ask serious questions way too early. They want to find out if the guy is serious about wanting a relationship, if the guy wants to get married, or if he wants kids.

Although it's understandable that a woman doesn't want to waste her time and wants to know whether the guy is serious or a player, asking serious questions early on is a serious turn-off. Come on, think about it, you haven't even got to know each other, the guy's not yet made up his mind about you, and you're discussing marriage and kids?

Even if you think you're being subtle about it, if a man suspects you're even thinking about marriage or kids, an image of a time bomb shaped like a baby will form in his mind. For the rest of the date each passing second will be about as comfortable as sitting in front of a time bomb watching the timer tick down.

How would you like it if on your first date a guy asked you, "So how long does a guy have to date you before you put out?" or "Do you know what the number sixty-nine denotes?" You're not going to like it. In fact you'll probably feel like slapping the guy and walking off. That's the level of discomfort a guy feels when a woman puts him on the spot, except he can't even slap a girl before walking away.

Lesson to be learned: a guy might not be playing around, but he doesn't want to feel like he's being evaluated on his marriage potential straight away. He doesn't want to feel like he's being interrogated. The two of you need to have some fun first and get to know each other.

I said early in the book that if you want to find out if a guy is a player or not, you just need to ask him to be in a monogamous relationship with you. But you can't do this on the first couple of dates! You only ask such a serious question when you're comfortable with one another, when it looks like there's a good chance the two of you will have sex.

The same goes for asking a guy about the future. You might not want to be with a guy who's not going to marry you or doesn't want kids, but you can't ask that within the first few months of the relationship. You might think that will save time, but it just comes off as desperate, and even if the guy does want to marry and have kids, you'll never know because you scared him off with the question.

Unfortunately when it comes to relationships, you can't push things too fast. You have to invest a certain amount of time in a guy, get him to feel comfortable, and get him to feel like he really wants you before asking more serious questions.

Being Bossed Around

I've worked in the finance industry, so I know a lot of very successful female investment bankers, lawyers, and women in powerful positions at work. A lot of these women often complain they have problems attracting men, and here's the reason:

Men want to date a woman . . . . not a man!

On a date a really strong minded and independent woman often communicates in a way that challenges a guy, to the point where it sounds abrasive.

Although men appreciate accomplished women who are confident, they want to avoid getting into a relationship where they might be pushed around and controlled by their partner. I know, it's pathetic and we have fragile egos, but before you trash this book, you have to understand this is just part of male psychology.

Our preferences exist as a result of our very nature, so while society has changed and there are more and more successful women, we are still attracted to women that have a feminine and nurturing demeanor. What we prefer in the opposite sex cannot be changed. If I reversed the roles and acted in a feminine manner, and turned up at a date in a skirt, then most women will equally be turned off.

Lesson to be learned: The problem isn't a woman that is successful. The problem is in the communication. When we go on a date we want to leave everything behind and have fun. We want a woman that can turn us on, not a boss that will chew us out. So a girl should let her hair down, learn to flirt, and just have some fun.

Men might not like needy women, but they also don't want someone that will dominate them either. Decent men want to be with an equal partner, and this is where finding the right balance is really important.

High Maintenance

If you're looking for a smart guy, then you also have to appreciate the fact that men in general are very wary of women who come across as high maintenance or gold diggers, and smart men can sense when a woman puts too much emphasis on a man's earning power.

Decent guys have no problems being a provider, and they know money is important. But they don't want to date women who will leave them the minute they lose their jobs or have a period of hardship. In other words they want to be loved for who they really are, and they want to have a partner that will be with them through the good and the bad.

Every woman wants to be loved for who she is, so I'm sure women understand this. Women hate to feel like they're being viewed as a sex object, so women should understand that men hate to feel like they're being used as an ATM machine.

If you ask around, very few women will admit they're materialistic or will only date a man if a man fits a certain financial criteria. But in reality a lot of the women who say they're not picky give off the vibes that they're high maintenance, especially on the first couple of dates.

Here are a few ways to turn men off.

1) Expect the man to pay for pretty much everything on a date. Most men are probably okay with paying for the first date, as well as the majority of expenses on subsequent dates. But if you never offer to pay for anything, then the guy could start worrying. I personally think if the guy pays three quarters on a date and the girl pays a quarter, that's a good balance.

2) Ask too many questions that try to garner information about the guy's financial situation. Questions that a girl conceives as subtle like "What type of car do you drive?" don't come across as subtle at all and can be taken in the wrong way.

3) Let a man feel that you have extremely expensive tastes or a lavish lifestyle before he's even gotten to know you. It's especially bad if a woman comes to the date wearing really expensive brands, orders really expensive stuff on the menu and then sits there expecting the guy to pay.

Lesson to be learned: If you're going to gold dig, be smart about it! Just kidding.

Actually, I'm not. If you're going to gold dig, be smart about it!

It's a really bad idea to try and find out about a guy's financial situation immediately, and it's a bad idea to make a guy bear most of the expenditures in the early stages of dating. I'm not saying that no men are willing to bear such costs. A lot of rich men love to surround themselves with women who have expensive tastes; these women are called trophy wives, and mistresses.

But if you're already finding it hard to meet a decent guy, and finally you go on a date with a guy who's great in many ways, wouldn't it be a shame if he's scared off because of some misunderstanding over money?

You might want reassurance that you're not wasting time on a guy who's broke, but you need to be patient in order to find out this information. Don't put men on the spot too soon when it comes to money, or you might scare away the decent ones.

Chapter 20

Never Hurt a Man's Ego

I know the title of the chapter is going to sound bad to some women, but let me explain myself. There are five things men are really sensitive about: their careers, their standing with their peers, their height, the amount of hair left on their heads, and their sexual prowess.

The average man's pride is linked to these five things, and a man's pride is one of the most important things in his life. Men have fought wars and killed each other over ego, that's how important (and stupid) our pride is to us. If you hurt a man's feelings with regards to these five things, and you make him feel emasculated enough (aka pussy whipped, aka you say jump, he asks how high), then resentment will start to brew and he could well walk away from the relationship in future.

There are a few things that I've observed women do that are a big no-no when it comes to men. I'm not saying all men get butt-hurt in the following situations; some men are thick skinned, and others get upset over little things. But it's just not a good idea to risk these actions.

Never Make a Man Feel Like He's Crap in Bed

I never have to face this problem because I'm so damn good in bed . . . . nah, just kidding.

I mentioned earlier that men like it when women are responsive in bed. The reason that men like this is because they want to feel they're good enough to make a woman feel good. In other words, every man secretly wants to think he's a stud in bed (even if he's not). Flip this around, and you can do real damage to a man's pride if you make him feel he's not desired and is crap in bed. In fact if you want to break up with a man, the fastest way to do this is to tell him he's crap in bed and that he's got a small dick.

Never Chastise a Man in Public

No matter how badly a guy messes up or pisses you off, if he's in front of your mutual friends or people who know him, never chastise him or make him look bad. He's not a child, and you don't want him to lose face in front of others. Give him an evil look and let him know you're pissed off, but save the lecture for the car or when you get home. You can rip his head off later for whatever transgression that occurred.

Never Talk about a Man's Insecurities

If he's got a problem with hair loss, his career, or anything else, and he's visibly upset but doesn't want to talk about it, then just leave it. There's no upside to it. It's just like how there's no upside for a man to discuss a woman's weight or her age with her; it's not going to make her feel better, and there's a risk it'll just upset her or piss her off.

I know this one guy who tried to give my female friend constructive criticism about her weight. He told her that if she lost some weight, she'll attract more men, and she totally flipped out on him. The same thing goes for issues that are insecurities for men. If he doesn't want to talk about it, don't bother trying to make a guy feel better; just leave it alone, and he'll deal with it himself in his own way.

Never Flash Your Career Success in a Man's Face

You can brag about your career, but only if the guy's equally or more successful. If you're more successful than your man, don't flaunt it in his face. I'm almost cringing because I know some women are going to read this and totally flip out. I can just imagine there's one reader thinking:

"Why should I feed a man's ego? I do as I please, and if I want to celebrate my success, that's my right. I worked hard all my life to get where I am and I do as I please. Who are you to tell me what I can or cannot do? Men aren't better than women, you chauvinistic asshole!"

She's right too. Men aren't better than women these days. Loads of women now kick men's butts at work. But that's work. If you want harmony in your relationship, and not resentment that's brewing below the surface only to bite you in the ass years later, then don't make a man feel like a failure when it comes to his career.

You might want to do what you like, but that's doesn't change male psychology; it doesn't change the fact that men are driven to seek power and success at work, and it makes them feel bad when they think they're not good enough and their own woman has them beat. Some women have to understand that even as society progresses, human nature never changes.

Cater to His Ego to Get What You Want

If you want true control in your relationship, then make your man feel like he's got power. If you want to make sure that your man treats you well and loves you, that everything in the relationship is rosy then don't compete with your man in every area of life.

Women who don't understand male psychology try to go head-to-head with their men; they don't get that men and women are naturally different. At work it should be all about head-to-head competition, but not in a relationship.

Using your femininity to get what you want doesn't make you weak; it just means you're using your own natural strengths. Using your feminine powers of persuasion is a much more effective strategy than getting in a man's face. Give you an example.

When my friend Lisa first started dating her husband, Mark, she had a hang-up about him because he wasn't making enough money. She earned almost double what he made. In fact Mark struggled financially just to woo her and to stay in her life. But she could tell he really loved her, so she started catering to his ego. Instead of nagging him or making him feel even more powerless about his career, she told him he was smart enough and good enough to do better, and when a good job opportunity came up, she encouraged him to go in that direction.

Many years later Mark has worked his way up the new company; he's a director at the firm and earns more than her. They now have a big house, and he's the main bread-winner. At the end of the day, who cares what method Lisa used? Mark feels like the man, but Lisa was the one that was truly controlling the situation. They're living in a bigger house, and they have a happy family.

She got what she wanted by using the most effective strategy, by feeding her man's ego. Being equals in a relationship doesn't mean you have to be equals in every aspect of the relationship. Hey, what can I say? I'm not only an asshole, I'm an ignorant and chauvinistic asshole . . . . but I still understand how men work.

Chapter 21

Stuff That Pisses Women Off

In the last couple of chapters I've mentioned some of the things that women do that might scare men off or upset them. The reason I mention them is because a lot of break ups happen after small misunderstandings turn into resentment, and then that resentment causes a loss in attraction or fighting.

It pays to know what turns men off to avoid these misunderstandings. It also pays to understand some of the things that men do that turn women off, so I'm going to come out as a representative for all mankind and explain why we do some really annoying shit that pisses women off. Remember, I'm just the messenger, so don't hate me for it!

Your Man Falls Asleep Right After Sex

Men often fall asleep after sex, whereas women generally stay alert and get pissed off the man's falling asleep. Hell, I think I've fallen asleep a few times in the middle of a blowjob, and it's got to suck giving a blowjob to a guy that's snoring.

This causes a lot of problems in the bedroom. After sex, a woman is still alert and wants to talk or get a hug, but her man's snoring away already, so she starts feeling like he's an inconsiderate bastard and is just using her for sex.

Men don't do this on purpose; we're not deliberately trying to be insensitive. Falling asleep is a result of our physiology. Sex for a woman has a big emotional component to it, but for men sex is more physical, and sex helps remove a lot of the stress and tension that a man feels. When a man has an orgasm his brain releases a cocktail of chemicals that creates sexual satisfaction and a soothing effect. This relaxes the guy, his brain shuts down, and if he's already tired from work, it has the effect of sending him straight to sleep.

Male physiology can't be changed, so there's no easy fix for women out there. It just pays to know why it happens so you don't get pissed off. I guess if you're really pissed off, you could always buy one of those spanking paddles from the sex toy shop, and spank him when he falls asleep.

There's another theory offered by my friend Amy as to why men fall asleep after sex and women don't. She said, "Women also feel sleepy after an orgasm. The problem is that most men finish in about half the time it takes for a women to climax, so the women is left lying there twiddling her thumbs."I actually believe that. But hey, don't get mad at us for sucking, okay?

When Men Are Stressed out but Don't Talk

When a woman is stressed out or emotionally distressed, areas of the brain that are responsible for speech functions will become more active, and she'll start talking to relieve stress. It's what women do.

In fact this book exists only because I've had dozens of women complain to me about their asshole boyfriends, and when women complain about their boyfriends, I've realized they're usually not looking for an effective solution to the problem; most of the time a girl who's distressed just wants to be heard.

The solution is usually pretty simple:

Girl 1: My boyfriend is selfish.
Solution: He's an asshole; dump his sorry ass!

Girl 2: My boyfriend cheated on me.
Solution: He's an asshole; dump his sorry ass!

Girl 3: My boyfriend is really mean to me and makes me feel crap.
Solution: He's an asshole; dump his sorry ass!

The solution to the problem is often very clear to me, and I'll tell the girl, but she'll just keep talking and talking because she's distressed and just wants to be heard.

Men on the other hand are totally different. When we are stressed out and bothered about something, we try to solve the problems in our heads; our focus goes to that problem, and we find it hard to listen or to talk. In fact we'll shut everything else out in order to give the problem our full attention.

A man doing this can often piss off his wife or girlfriend, because she starts to wonder why he's distressed but not talking to her. It looks like he's trying to shut her out. In her mind he either doesn't trust her, doesn't love her enough to share with her, or is pissed off with her. But it's got nothing to do with that.

When we're stressed out, we retreat into our own little bubble. So if you see your man stressed out but not talking to you, don't worry, he's got nothing against you. If you try to get to him he's only going to get pissed off and tell you to go away. The best thing you can do is to just leave him alone.

Your Man's Being a Moron

Right now I can just picture girls reading this book, looking across the living room at their man, nodding, and thinking, "Oh yeah, my man's a moron."

Women often see men zone out in front of the TV, play computer games for hours on end, or do other moronic things that make them look totally brain dead, and women don't get how men can act like that. In fact women sometimes get pissed off at men for seemingly zoning out. It just irritates the crap out of women to see a man do absolutely nothing, when the man could be doing more productive things like helping around the house or listening to her talk!

What women don't get is that when men try to relax, a large part of our brains shuts down, and it's possible for a man to sit on a couch for hours on end like a moron, thinking about absolutely nothing at all besides the TV. Women on the other hand have much more active brains even when relaxed. Women think all the time, so women can't relate, and can't stand it when they see the man they're with vegetating in the living room.

But unfortunately you can't change this. It's just the way we are; it's the way we relax. So on behalf of all mankind, I would like to apologize for us acting like morons. Don't take it personally.

Your Man Doesn't Listen to You

When a man first starts to chase a woman, he's usually listening, and that's because out on a date the guy's always alert. Once in a relationship, however, you'll witness a man when he's actually relaxing. When he's in his zoned-out state, he's practically brain dead and can't hear a frigging thing. If you say anything to him when he's zoned out, the 20 percent of his brain that is functioning might register and he'll probably nod, but in fact what you said went in one ear and straight out the other. When a woman tries to get her husband to do something around the house, what she says and what he hears are totally different.

The woman says:

"Robert.... ROBERT! I thought I told you to do the damn laundry! Why is there dirty laundry all over the floor? Robert? Robert, are you even listening to me?"

You know what Robert hears?

"Robert .... ROBERT! Blah, blah, blah .... blah .... blah .... blah, blah, blah .... blah Robert? Robert .... blah, blah, blah, blah, blah."

.... And then Robert will finally turn his head and say, "Baby, are you talking to me?"

Have you been in this situation before?

If you have and want to avoid it happening ever again, if you want him to do something, then here's what you do.

You totally ignore him and give him the silent treatment. Now, if he's an attuned and sensitive guy, he'll pick up on it after, say, two hours, and he'll naturally come to talk to you and ask you what's wrong.

Or you could do this:

If you want him to hear you loud and clear, then you wait until you're in bed with him. Then when he snuggles up to you and wants to have sex, you turn around and look him in the eye, and you give him the most evil look you've ever given another human being .... and then you point at the washing machine ....

Chapter 22

Drawing Your Boundaries

Human beings are selfish creatures; in fact we can be downright evil. The reason we have cops on the streets and a legal system is because if we didn't, it'd take just a matter of days or weeks for society to totally fall apart and for anarchy to reign.

When it comes to your relationship, you need to lay the law down early as well. You need some "dick control" so to speak. Set boundaries or else you'll get anarchy in your relationship. Even if a guy is a decent guy and has integrity, he might step out of line sometimes.

Women who don't lay the law down early will let their men get away with things because they don't want to upset their men. But then later in the relationship, when the woman tries to regain control, it's too late. The man's used to misbehaving, and that's when resentment starts and fights break out.

I know there'll be girls out there saying, "Well if my man loves me, why can't he just behave?" Ladies, think of it this way: most kids love their parents, but most kids break rules and create havoc all the time, so they need to be disciplined. Though your man isn't a kid, he's still human and will break some of your rules, and if you don't come down on him, then he'll get spoiled and start taking you for granted.

Set boundaries to protect yourself as soon as you can. Boundaries are basically limits you set in a relationship to protect yourself. If a man crosses your boundaries, then you have to let him know it's not acceptable. If a man crosses your boundaries repeatedly, it's a clear sign that he's a selfish asshole, and you should leave him.

Healthy boundaries include things such as:

- Being honest with one another. A man who's lying to you is crossing this.
- Respecting the differences in a partner. This works both ways, so again, don't try to change your man into what you what him to be.
- Commitment to one another. Cheating is an obvious crossing of this boundary.
- Balancing intimacy and personal space. Not enough intimacy or being in each other's face all the time and not having personal time and freedom crosses this line.

Basically, boundaries are things that matter to you in a relationship, and I can't list them all for you. It's not hard to figure out what your boundaries are. Whenever the other person does something that upsets you and you think they're being selfish, that becomes a boundary.

Effective Communication

Figuring what your boundaries are is easy. Enforcing them is not, because there are certain forms of communication to which men do not respond well.

Nagging (God please save me from this crazy woman!)

Nagging is probably the worst way to communicate displeasure with a man, because quite frankly, *it's fucking annoying*!

Whenever a woman nags a man and shows displeasure in her voice, the man immediately feels like he's eight again and being scolded by his mother, and men hate this feeling. In fact men hate this feeling so much it's one of the reasons we try to get our independence as soon as possible. The day we leave home to live on our own for the first time is one of the happiest days of our lives simply because we no longer have to face the constant nagging.

Nagging doesn't bring a man closer to you. It makes you sound like his mother, and that's an immediate turn off.

Getting Emotional (Oh no, please don't!)

A lot of women tend to get visibly emotional when they're telling a man he's in the wrong. In fact I know women who cry on purpose because they think this gets the man to feel worse. It actually doesn't work that way. If you get all emotional in front of a man, he might say he's sorry and try to comfort you at the time, but that's just to get you to stop crying. Deep down it makes the man so uncomfortable he wants to immediately bolt out of the room.

Crying and getting emotional in front of a man just makes you look weak and unattractive to the man, and, in the long run, works against you.

Be Business-like (Civilized)

If you observe men when they are not happy with each other, you'll see that they communicate their displeasure in an almost business like way (and, if that doesn't work, we start punching each other).

Men talk in this way because when it's between guys, we don't want to look weak. It's also much easier to communicate and deal with a person who's not emotional. If you ever watch cops confront a distressed individual, the first thing they say is, "Sir, calm down."

If you want to speak to a man in a language that he understands, then the best way to communicate displeasure is to be concise and be business-like. In fact it's the same way a good parent educates a kid.

Walk Away (Effective)

Let's imagine your man lied to you about something, and you're upset. What's one of the most effective strategies to get him to feel sorry and to stop doing it?

You get in your car and drive away. You go out with your girlfriends, and when the guy gets home, he'll start to wonder where you are. When he calls you up, you tell him, "I know you lied, but I'm not going to deal with it now; I'm with my girls having fun. We'll talk about it when I get home."

Now, this might seem like running away from the problem and seems immature, but it'll only come across that way if you get emotional. If you're cool or even cold about it when you talk to him, it scares the crap out of the guy. It makes him worry that you're going to leave him, and this makes him behave immediately. In fact he'll probably start freaking out on the phone. "Wait, baby, wait, let me just explain. Baby, wait, don't hang up!" *Click* . . . . Dick control at its finest.

Just remember to be business-like when you do get home. Tell him in a concise manner why you're not happy with him lying, and avoid getting emotional.

The Ultimate Threat

Getting cold and driving away from a man brings me to my next tool, the ultimate threat. During the cold war, the Soviet Union and the United States were enemies for forty years, but they never went to war with each other. You want to know why?

They never went to war because they had nuclear weapons, they had the ultimate threat, and they knew if they went to war, then they'd totally destroy each other, so they avoided war at all costs.

You can have an ultimate threat, too. That threat is letting your man know that if he did something really bad then you won't hesitate to leave him. This is different from a bluff or an empty threat. I know women who threaten to leave their men, and then when the guys do something really bad like cheat, the women put up with it. Then things get worse because the men know the women are just bluffing.

The ultimate threat only works if in your mind you are truly willing to make the commitment to leave the man if he hurts you bad enough. I know men who would never cheat on their wives, would never hit their wives, and would never hurt their wives badly, not only because they're decent men, but because they know if they did cross that line, then their wives would leave them forever.

The ultimate threat is not something you want to use, but it's something you want to have in back up, because when it exists, the man will behave and that right there is ultimate dick control!

Chapter 23

Being on the Same Team

I've had girls complain to me that no matter what they do, they can never make their man happy. They're there for their guy when he's upset. They have sex with their man when he wants it. They basically bend over backward for the guy, and still he treats them like dirt.

This happens because they were never on the same team. The guy was an asshole and started chasing after the girl for sex only; he never had the intention of being in an equal relationship. The only person in an asshole's team is himself, and when you put an asshole with a nice girl, the nice girl comes last every time. Sometimes it helps to see things from a simplistic point of view, because the answer is staring you right in the face.

If you want a relationship, and the guy just wants sex, he's not on your team and is wasting your time.

If you want happily ever after, and the guy just wants to drink beer, party, and stay single for the next twenty years, he's not on your team.

If you want fidelity in your relationship, and the guy cheats on you, he's not on your team.

Treating someone well only has positive effects if you're on the same team and your interests are aligned with each other. If you're with an asshole, no matter what you do he won't really appreciate it. In fact if you're having relationship problems, then ask yourself if it feels like the two of you are on the same team. If you can't honestly say that, then you should cut the guy off. Save time and energy by throwing all his shit out of the house, and put a sign on the front lawn that says, "I bought a big dog and I'm training it to rip your nuts off!"

Working together is vital if you want your relationship to be healthy and long lasting. Sure, even couples that love each other argue from time to time. But whenever couples stop being on the same team, being together will become intolerable.

You can easily tell if the guy's on your side. For one thing he won't be crossing your boundaries all the time, he'll care about what you think, and he'll always make sure that you're happy. But being on the same team is a two-way thing, and I've seen a lot of women treat their men like dirt, too. Sometimes there's so much miscommunication between a couple, they start hating each other, even though they originally had each other's best interests in mind.

If you want your guy to think you're really special, and you want to keep the guy interested in the long run, then there are some effective ways to show your affection. Not all men respond the same way, but a decent man will definitely appreciate the following.

Back Him Up

Real men don't like to be mothered, and they don't need to be assisted all the time for every little thing that comes up in life, but they do like it when they feel they've got their woman's backing.

My friend Wendy and her boyfriend constantly back each other up. There have been times when her boyfriend was insulted in public by someone and things got heated, and she'd step in with comments to put the other guy down and back her boyfriend up, not in a way that made him look weak, but just to offer a few accurate points and get the other guy to shut up. What was being argued wasn't important, the important thing was that when other people messed with her man, she stood by his side.

Show the Guy You Care

Showing your man that you care is different from smothering him with affection. When needy people do nice things for the people they like, you can often see a sort of anticipation on their faces. It's like they're doing nice things in the hope that nice things will be done in return. People who are in a healthy relationship often do nice things out of the blue, just to show they care, but expect nothing in return. A former colleague of mine told me how he really loved it when his wife would pack some of his favorite snacks for him every time he had to go on a business trip. It was a small gesture but it made him appreciate how thoughtful his wife was.

Being Willing to Disagree for His Benefit

Some women don't push their men enough and allow their men to get lazy and slack off because they don't want to get confrontational with them. Other women get too confrontational and come off as a drill sergeant that's barking orders.

If you really want a guy to feel like you're on his side, the best way is to gently push the guy so that he succeeds in what he does without feeling pressured. For example, if a guy's drinking too much and not eating well, let him know in a casual and caring manner. If the guy has a problem at work or with his career, and you have a solution in mind, share it with him, because your opinion could possibly solve his problem. He's not a child and doesn't need to be lectured, but if you remind him of his faults, he'll know that you're looking out for him.

The key is to understand what your man responds to best, because different men respond to different forms of communication. Figure out what your guy likes and then show your love in a way that he will respond to. If you can really show that you're on the same team as the guy, then you will have accomplished the last step in getting a man to fall in love with you: he'll start to feel that his life is better with you in it than without you.

Chapter 24

Fun and Spontaneity

So now you've got your man. You've made sure he's decent and not playing games. You've made sure you're not pissing each other off, and you've got good dick control. What now? Now you make the relationship interesting so you don't get bored with one another.

I've never been married, but I've been in a relationship long enough to know that after many years, things can really get boring. I've also seen relationships that have fallen apart after many years, so I know that boredom is a reality that can't be ignored.

Most of the time people don't even intend for things to become boring; it just happens. Work can get in the way of the home life. People come home tired and stressed out, or they're moody and hardly fun to be with. Some people spend all their time and energy raising their children, and before long they're no longer in love with their spouse, and the only thing holding them together are the kids.

The best way to avoid this happening to you is to always make an effort to make things fun and spontaneous, no matter how long you're been with a person. Routines will get tiresome if there's never any change. You might not be able to mix things up every day, but you want to do so frequently enough so that life is still an adventure and you're still looking forward to being with your partner.

Here are some of the things you can practically do at any time. They require little effort, but shouldn't be done every day or they too would become a routine:

1) For no apparent reason what so ever, grab your man, give him a passionate kiss, and tell him how much you love him.

2) An alternative is to grab the back of his head and say, "Fuck the shit out of me, now!" That'll surprise him too!

3) If you only eat out, make the effort to cook a nice dinner, or vice versa.

4) Instead of letting the man shower alone, hop in the shower with him. It's a fun bonding experience.

5) Have a date night once a week, where you try and make it feel like you're dating for the first time. Instead of going casual, you both take the time to get dressed up like you would for a proper date.

6) Hold your partner's hand no matter how many years you've been together. It might seem trivial, but in fact it increases intimacy. It's actually shocking how many couples start off holding hands and then don't do it after a while.

7) If your partner has been stressed from work, bring out a bottle of massage oil. Once in a while a good massage is a good way of having an intimate experience.

8) Have a common interest that both of you do together. For example, go cycling together on weekends; it's healthy and fun and you get to stay in shape together.

9) Leave a note for your man telling him how much you love him, hidden in a place he wouldn't expect, like inside his briefcase.

10) Dress up in something naughty once in a while to spice up your love life. It could be lingerie or a uniform.

There are other options that cost money and can't be done all the time, but they can be great bonding experiences. Anything that has an adventurous element to it tends to help bonding, because the unusual or exciting aspect of it will heightens the senses.

1) Get together on Friday right after work, and then drive or fly somewhere for the weekend. It could be a beach resort or a campsite out in the middle of nowhere, or go visit a city with a lively night life.

2) Try doing some crazy stuff together. Exciting experiences can bring people closer together, so I would suggest things that will get the adrenaline pumping. Go white water rafting or sky diving together. If that's too intense, then go horseback riding or rock climbing together.

The opportunities are endless, and if you have kids, all you need is a dependable baby-sitter.

I don't buy the crap when people say they're too tired or busy to do more things with their partners. That's like saying they're too tired and busy to live; it's just a lame excuse, and everyone can make a relationship more exciting with a little more effort.

The only barrier to success is yourself.

Chapter 25

Date Your Best Friend

This is the last chapter of the book, and I hope you enjoyed it. I apologize if I was vulgar and politically incorrect, after all, I am an asshole. I'll end the book by sharing with you some personal thoughts about what a proper relationship should be.

When I started writing this book, I was lonely and guilt ridden. Now I'll explain why many months ago I found myself in Nepal looking to freeze to death on a mountain.

I didn't set out to do that. I went to Nepal to clear my mind and to think, but as I sat on that mountain, I started thinking about my ex-girlfriend. I realized that not only had I lost a woman who loved me, I had also lost my best friend. When we were together, I was able to be myself in front of her without worrying I would be judged. I was able to show my weak side without fearing that I would be laughed at or looked down upon. When I was at the lowest point of my life, she was there for me.

I had found someone whom I could truly open up to. I had found my best friend, and I threw it all away because I was too selfish to appreciate her, and now there's no going back. She's gone forever, and I have to live with that.

Guilt and regret are the worst feelings to have in life.

But from my messed-up experiences, I hope I at least learned something. I realize now a lot of people are unhappy in their relationships because they don't understand what relationships should be about.

We live in a cruel and narcissistic world, and many people go into relationships thinking about themselves. "What can I get? What is this person providing for me?"

We're so caught up with ourselves that we don't know what love really means anymore. Love isn't about the chemistry we feel when we first meet someone. It's not about the first impressions and the interesting conversations. Sure, we need to feel attracted, and we need our partners to feel attracted to us.

But once you're in a relationship, it's about more than just the stuff I put in the first twenty-four chapters of this book. You will only be happy (and your relationship will only work) in the long run if the man you're with is your best friend in addition to being your lover.

A good relationship should have excitement and chemistry, and it should be about fun and spontaneity. But a good relationship is also about treating someone right, patience, and selflessness, the type of things best friends offer each other.

When I see girls dating assholes these days, I feel really sorry for them. Not in a condescending way, but because I know they're dating men like myself, and I just want to tell them life's too short to date men like me.

When I see how badly some of these men treat their women, I get angry. Not because I have a right to judge, but because I see one person who's longing and hoping for love, but stuck with someone who's perverse and knows nothing about love.

So my last piece of advice is this: don't just rely on feelings, and don't long for love so badly that you go blind. Life is short and you can't waste it dating selfish assholes. Find a good man, a man with integrity, a man who will treat you well, and above all else a man who will be your best friend. I wish you all the best, and I hope you find the man and the love that you deserve.

Frequently Asked Questions

In the process of writing this book and interviewing hundreds of women, there were some questions that either came up frequently or that I found interesting, so I'm going to share them with you in case you find them helpful with your own situation. If you have more questions, or you want to read my blog and get advice on your relationship then please visit www.playersbegone.com

Q: Women often play men too. Why did you only write about men mistreating women?

A: Yes, I know women can mistreat men as well. But because I'm not a woman I can't write a book called Life's Too Short to Date Women Like Me. I'll let you know when I get a sex change though!

Q: I don't want to be so emotional and needy in front of my boyfriend, but I can't seem to help being that way. I was never like this with other guys. My question is how does a girl go about controlling her emotions?

A: There are two reasons people act needy in a relationship. (1) Generally if one person is more in love and the other person doesn't care as much, then neediness tends to appear because the person who's in love wants to get more attention and affection. If you are needy in this situation and the guy doesn't care, then the guy's an asshole and not treating you well. There's not much you can do other than to communicate your need for more affection. If nothing changes, it's best to cut your losses and find a guy who will treat you well.

2) If a person is insecure and lacks self-esteem then that person might act needy, in which case I suggest that person needs to learn to be happy on his or her own. A person shouldn't rely on a partner for happiness. People should learn to be happy hanging out with friends, doing things that bring them pleasure, and have a positive attitude toward life. However if you aren't needy with other men, then I doubt that's the case here.

Q: How do you defeat a man who knows how to play relationship games and knows how to hold back his feelings and love for you?

A: "Defeat"? There is no defeating selfishness! As for a man who isn't showing his feelings or love for you, have you ever considered he's in a relationship but not in love? There are mind games you can play that create attraction in the short term, but can you really maintain the game playing for the rest of your life? Accept the guy for who he is or leave him. You can't be happy if you have to resort to playing games for the rest of your life, and I'm pretty sure the relationship will fail in the end.

Q: My boyfriend goes out five times a week. He's not cheating, but all his friends are party animals, so he's always staying out real late. How do I make a guy not go out as much without making him feel suffocated or annoyed?

A: To get a guy to go out less, you give him a really good blowjob and then tell him he won't get any more if he goes out the rest of the week! Alternatively, you accept the guy isn't ready to settle down and is in fact a party animal. I used to go party all the time just like your boyfriend. I go out a lot less now because I mellowed out. I guess I just got old or bored of going out so much, but it came naturally and wasn't enforced.

Q: How many days a week do you think a couple should get together in order to maintain a healthy relationship?

A: At the beginning I don't think a girl should see a guy more than twice a week, simply because it's a good idea to play hard to get. After a couple is steadily dating, though, I don't see why they can't see each other daily; after all, marriage usually means being together every day. If seeing each other is already a burden in the dating stage, then forget about ever getting married.

Q: My boyfriend cheated on me, and he promised never to do it again. Can I trust him?

A: They say once a cheater, always a cheater. Though I don't think this is always true, I will say that most cheaters will cheat again because it's in their nature. Some cheaters will move on to a new relationship and won't cheat again in that particular relationship. But generally if a man's cheated in a relationship, it's likely he'll do it again and again to the same woman, no matter what the promises are.

Q: Maybe you're right. My boyfriend's not treating me right. But I love him so much and just don't feel strong enough to leave this man. What can I do?

A: This is a problem shared by a lot of women. I feel that when women (or men for that matter) are in love with another person who's not treating them well, their behavior will start to resemble a person that's addicted to a drug.

Quitting any sort of addiction isn't easy; there's always a painful withdrawal process, or it wouldn't be an addiction in the first place. The only way to make it easier is to admit you have a problem on your hands. Stop finding excuses for the guy and accept that he will never change and will always hurt you.

Before you met the man, I'm sure you were looking for happiness in your life. If you're not feeling happy now, then it's time to move on, even if the pain is significant. When you do leave the man, the pain won't last forever. It's only then that you will have the chance to find true happiness.

Q: My husband stopped having sex with me. Why has this happened, and what can I do about it?

A: There are multiple reasons for why a man stops having sex with his woman. It might not have anything to do with you. Stress can be a huge factor, so if he's stressed out at work, he could lose his sex drive. Illness could also be a factor; it's a good idea to go see a doctor in this case. The doctor will prescribe medication and give you advice on how to reduce your partner's stress level.

The other reason could be that he's lost interest. Sex is a good barometer of the relationship, and if your relationship has become dull in general, then he could lose interest in bed as well. A good idea is to try and spice things up again; refer to chapter twenty-three. If that fails, then I suggest getting help from a therapist.

Q: I'm a single mother, and I find that men will immediately lose interest in me when they find out I have a child. What can I do?

A: My mother was a single mother before she met my stepdad. I won't lie to you, trying to find a man when you already have a child is not easy, because most men are reluctant to take up the responsibility of looking after someone else's child. However many women with children get married, so it's not an impossibility.

The key is to make yourself look beautiful. Be happy with life and be confident with yourself. When you meet a man, don't care so much whether he likes you. If he doesn't like you, there are other men out there. If you become insecure about men walking away from you, it'll be reflected in needy behavior that the man will sense, and you'll scare him off. On the other hand, if you allow yourself to feel like you're hot stuff, allow yourself to be happy, and become a joy to be with, then a man will fall in love with you even if you have children.

Q: Why are men such dogs? When my daughter grows up I'm going to teach her that all men are assholes.

A: Wow, slow down! Telling your daughter that all men are assholes is the quickest way to screw up her life, and ironically it will probably get her attached to assholes because she'll think all men are like that. Not all men are dogs. There are men who treat women well and there are bad men. It's no different from any other area of life. We protect ourselves from strangers because some might hurt us or steal from us. Accepting there are good and bad people in this world is just part of life. We need to learn how to avoid the bad while retaining the good. Relationships are no different, and being jaded about men only makes things worse.

Q: I always date men who turn out to be jerks. What can I do about this?

A: Some women find nice guys boring because those guys smother them with attention, and these women need a man who's challenging in order to feel attraction. The problem is a lot of men who are challenging only act that way because they don't give a crap about the girl in the first place.

There's two ways to get around this. (1) Be more selective, avoid any selfish guys at the first sign of selfishness, and raise your own value in order to attract some decent men. (2) Find someone you might not have initial chemistry with, but someone who doesn't turn you off and is really into you, and take the time to get to know them. I have female friends that have dated jerks over and over again. Then one day some guy they normally would not have gone for showed up and treated the girl very well, and over time feelings developed.

You can't go for someone who repulses you, but if you don't give a guy a chance, then how will you know you'll never like him?

Q: I find I'm very dependent on my boyfriend for happiness and tend to get very jealous and insecure when he's not with me or interacting with other girls. What can I do?

A: If the guy is interacting inappropriately with other girls, flirting with them or hanging out excessively with a particular girl, or even making physical contact with them in front of you, then it's totally normal to feel jealous and insecure because the guy is not respecting you. If this is the case you have to let the guy know that he's crossing one of your boundaries, and you have to be willing to leave the guy if he doesn't stop.

If the guy isn't doing anything inappropriate, but you find yourself constantly feeling insecure, then you could have a self-esteem issue. In a healthy relationship people should have their own time and space, and that includes your boyfriend. When he's having his alone time and is with his friends, you should be out with your friends and having fun with them. Don't sit at home alone, or you will start to feel left out and lonely. If you can't shake the insecure feeling no matter what, then it might also be a good idea to speak to a professional for advice.

Q: My boyfriend has a foot fetish. Is this normal, and what should I do about it? [Note: This has nothing to do with assholes, but a couple of girls asked about this and I found it amusing.]

A: Foot fetish is the most common fetish around, though a lot of people have other forms of fetishes. There are many reasons why people have fetishes, and I can't list them all. The most important thing is does it turn you off, or are you okay with it? If it's not a turn-off, then stop worrying about it. Like I said, a lot of people have fetishes, and your guy isn't some sort of weirdo. If you can't stand it and it's a total turn-off then I think you need to have an honest chat, and if he really needs it as part of his sex life and you can't deal with it, then it's better to break up rather than stay in a situation where before parties are unhappy.

Q: My boyfriend was really sweet when we first started dating, but recently he has become very possessive and controlling. What can I do?

A: If it bothers you, then you have to let him know immediately that he's crossing your boundaries. If you let him start acting in this way it could become a habit. Controlling and possessive behavior could show that the guy is insecure and is worried that you don't love him enough or might find someone else. It could also be something worse, such as an early sign of someone who could potentially be abusive.

If the guy doesn't stop being controlling even when you've told him that you can't stand it, then why stay in the relationship?

Q: My boyfriend isn't very romantic. What can I do?

A: Some men just aren't very romantic and find it hard to be overtly intimate. But ask yourself this: Is the guy selfish? Does he belittle you and make you feel bad about yourself? Is he stringing you along and refusing to settle down with you? If he's a narcissist or is afraid of commitment, then there's nothing you can do but cut your losses early. If he's just not that romantic but treats you well, are you happy? If you're happy, then I don't think it's the end of the world, but maybe you can just tell him you'd like it if he could make more effort some-times.